KU-236-154

To Anne,

Drop the Pink Elephant

Best Wishes

What the papers say ...

'What a great book. I would have no hesitation in recommending this book to anyone.

'This book is a must-read for anybody in a client/customer-facing position. I think anyone who talks to other people could benefit from reading it.'
MARKETING Magazine

'If your DNA's short on charisma, here's a guide to charm heaven. Learn how to captivate your listeners and speak so people understand you better. An easy read with perky drawings and bullet point summaries.'
HER WORLD Magazine

'McFarlan's method for revolutionising communication ... is as relevant to how we relate to family and friends as it is to how to get the best from a workforce.'
THE HERALD

'Even if you normally steer clear of self-help books, do try the very funny and perceptive Drop the Pink Elephant by Scottish television presenter Bill McFarlan.'
CALEDONIA

'It is very rare that anything that is good for you is also fun ... This book, however, is enormously pleasurable to read and the words of wisdom sink in without a murmur.'
CITY TO CITIES

'... it goes on to tackle every aspect of personal communication in a crisp, entertaining style. Plain English supporters will be particularly interested in chapters dealing with jargon (especially unfamiliar abbreviations) and grammar.'
PLAIN ENGLISH Magazine

'This is a fascinating must-read.'
GLASGOW EVENING TIMES

Drop the Pink Elephant

15 ways to say what you mean
— and mean what you say

BILL McFARLAN

CAPSTONE

© Bill McFarlan 2003, 2004

The right of Bill McFarlan to be identified as the author of this book has been asserted in accordance with the Copyright, Designs and Patents Act 1988

First edition published 2003
This edition published 2004 by
Capstone Publishing Limited (a Wiley Company)
The Atrium
Southern Gate
Chichester
West Sussex
PO19 8SQ
www.wileyeurope.com
E-mail (for orders and customer service enquiries): cs-books@wiley.co.uk

Reprinted November 2004, March 2005, October 2005, September 2006, December 2006, November 2007, March 2010, August 2011, March 2012, June 2013, February 2014, April 2015

All Rights Reserved. No part of this publication may be reproduced, stored in a retrieval system or transmitted in any form or by any means, electronic, mechanical, photocopying, recording, scanning or otherwise, except under the terms of the Copyright, Designs and Patents Act 1988 or under the terms of a licence issued by the Copyright Licensing Agency Ltd, 90 Tottenham Court Road, London W1T 4LP, UK, without the permission in writing of the Publisher. Requests to the Publisher should be addressed to the Permissions Department, John Wiley & Sons Ltd, The Atrium, Southern Gate, Chichester, West Sussex PO19 8SQ, UK, or e-mailed to permreq@wiley.co.uk, or faxed to (+44) 1243 770571.

Designations used by companies to distinguish their products are often claimed as trademarks. All brand names and product names used in this book are trade names, service marks, trademarks or registered trademarks of their respective owners. The Publisher is not associated with any product or vendor mentioned in this book.

This publication is designed to provide accurate and authoritative information in regard to the subject matter covered. It is sold on the understanding that the Publisher is not engaged in rendering professional services. If professional advice or other expert assistance is required, the services of a competent professional should be sought.

CIP catalogue records for this book are available from the British Library and the US Library of Congress

ISBN 13: 978-1-84112-637-1 (PB)

Typeset in Meridien by
Sparks Computer Solutions Ltd, Oxford (www.sparks.co.uk)
Printed and bound in Great Britain by TJ International Ltd, Padstow, Cornwall

Substantial discounts on bulk quantities of Capstone Books are available to corporations, professional associations and other organizations.

For details telephone John Wiley & Sons on (+44) 1243 770441, fax (+44) 1243 770571 or e-mail corporatedevelopment@wiley.co.uk

Dedication

This book is dedicated to:

My dad and late mum, whose love and security taught me realistic optimism.

My wife Caroline, whose loving encouragement has guided me through triumph and setback alike for 25 years.

My children Victoria, Emma and Andrew, whose tolerance of my Pink Elephant obsession is a credit to each of them.

And to Johanna MacVicar, whose courage and optimism in the face of illness and adversity extended her short life, gave new hope to others and gave new life to two dozen strangers. Literally.

May they – and everyone who reads this – benefit from sharing that obsession.

And special thanks to Caroline and Victoria for their incisive proof-reading of this book to ensure it follows my principles on punctuation, grammar and clarity.

Thanks also to John Moseley and the entire Wiley-Capstone team for their belief in this book and the opportunity they have created to share my principles with the world.

About the Author

Bill McFarlan is a journalist, broadcaster and Managing Director of one of Britain's leading media consultancies.

He established The Broadcasting Business in 1989 to help individuals and businesses get their message to the world in a brighter, more positive and more vivid manner.

Since then, he's conducted more than a thousand media training and presentation skills courses in Britain, France, Spain, the USA, the Caribbean and Africa.

He's a regular speaker at conferences and passionate advocate of confidence-building techniques.

In tandem with his business life is a broadcasting career that began in radio in 1980 and took him through news presentation at Scottish Television to ten years with the BBC, anchoring

Breakfast News, Reporting Scotland, Sportscene and *World's Strongest Man*.

He's fronted sports programmes on three satellite channels and is a regular contributor to news and current affairs programmes.

Bill lives in Glasgow with his wife and three children.

The Broadcasting Business can be contacted at www.broadcastingbusiness.co.uk or on 0141 427 2545.

Contents

World's Top Ten Pink Elephants

Simply remove the word in **bold** letters to reveal the picture each phrase creates.

'I did **not** *have sexual relations with that woman, Ms Lewinsky.'*
US President Bill Clinton in January 1998 on his relationship with the White House intern. Ten months later he apologized for misleading the American people with what he said

'I did **not** *rape Ulrika. I would* **never** *rape anyone.'*
Well-known UK TV presenter, whose denials were quickly followed by further allegations from numerous women

'There can be **no** *whitewash at the White House.'*
US President Richard Nixon, who relinquished the presidency because of ... a whitewash at the White House

'Telling my story was **never** *about money.'*
Paul Burrell, former butler to Princess Diana, who sold his story to the Daily Mirror for a reported £300,000

'*This is* **not** *a war on Islam.*'
Tony Blair on the War on ... Terrorism

'*I must state once and for all that I am* **not** *(Prince) Harry's father.*'
James Hewitt on that growing resemblance between Princess Diana's younger son and her former lover

'*I'm* **not** *thick. I'm* **not** *a bimbo. And I'm* **not** *a tart.*'
Big Brother 2001 runner-up Helen Adams on herself. The audience drew its own conclusions

'*I* **don't** *do drugs. I* **don't** *drink and drive and I* **don't** *have five kids to three different women.*'
Former Scotland captain Colin Hendry, accused only of elbowing an opponent

'*Read my lips.* **No** *new taxes.*'
US President George Bush ... before he increased taxes

'*It did* **not** *happen. Gennifer Flowers' story is* **not** *true.*'
Bill Clinton again, who later admitted under oath that he did in fact have sex with Ms Flowers

Foreword

I've worked in TV almost all my working life and first met Bill when he joined the *Breakfast News* presentation team in 1991. It was clear back then that he analysed every word, every tone and every twitch of his own performance ... and that of his interviewees and colleagues.

I saw why when I joined him in presenting some communication skills courses. The insight he offered into what each participant said ... and what they meant ... was tremendous. And after adopting his rules, each person showed a remarkable improvement in their ability to get their message across. *Drop the Pink Elephant* captures those rules and puts them in a bottle for anybody wanting to make more impact in their lives by really connecting with other people. It's essential reading for everybody interested in creating a deeper understanding with their colleagues, clients, family and friends.

Eamonn Holmes

Introduction

We agonize over the words to choose in an important letter. Devising a report can give us writer's block. Even writing a postcard can concentrate our mind on choosing our words carefully.

But in conversations, words can come gushing out of our mouths with hardly a thought for the impact they'll have on their audience. We spend so much more time speaking to people than writing to them, yet we seldom give enough thought to the consequences of our choice of words.

This book sets out to change all that.

Drop the Pink Elephant draws its conclusions from what I've learned about communication in over a quarter of a century working in the media. It's based on my career in journalism, which started in local newspapers as a cub reporter and took me through radio into television, presenting news and sports programmes for the BBC, Sky Sports and Independent Television.

That taught me to write – and to talk and behave on camera – with the reaction of the audience considered in everything I did. From that experience, I set up a media consultancy that has advised many of Britain's leading companies on how to handle the communication of new orders, product launches, industrial action, plant closures – and, tragically, even deaths.

That is all very well. We are naturally inclined to watch what we say in formal communication. But so much of our communication at work and at play is informal. And it is here that the cracks begin to appear.

So I've had to struggle like everybody else with my human frailties that constantly test what I've learned – to establish whether I talk a good game through my work, or actually live it. From the many occasions on which I've got it horribly wrong – and there are many, as you'll see – I gladly share my experience. That's taught me, on reflection, where it went wrong and how to fix it. Applying the lessons will help you to avoid such pain.

Much of what I suggest is simple common sense. But most of us learn common sense from suffering from the nonsense of a bad experience. So the simple rules I'm suggesting will, if applied, help you through many a tricky situation with clients, colleagues, family and friends.

And while changing our behaviour is a slow and often painful experience – although essential if we are to grow as human beings – changing the way we talk to people is instantly achievable and highly rewarding. Indeed, it's a first necessary step to changing behaviour.

Each chapter covers a different area of improving the way you communicate, but all are related. For instance, being positive in your language leads to eliminating negatives and the baggage we bring into our conversation. Removing words that water down your message – words like 'hopefully', 'reasonably' and 'quite', 'I'll try' or 'I'll do my best' – increases the commitment of the message.

Choosing the right word at the right moment every time is impossible. But applying the simple rules of this book is easy. If there's one golden rule it's this: make sure you engage your brain before opening your mouth.

But it's like learning to drive a car. First, learn the theory of the Highway Code to understand the rules of the road. Next, put the rules into practice. This is, of course, where things go wrong.

Why? Almost certainly because the Highway Code was abandoned for a moment. As with driving, you will have bumps and scrapes when putting these rules into practice, often caused by the thoughtlessness of somebody else.

But be patient! And practise the rules at every opportunity. Practise them in job interviews, client meetings, over family dinners, with friends and colleagues. Use them at work, in the pub and at home. Apply them in the company of anyone and everyone with whom you interact. The more often you apply these rules, the more often you'll communicate effectively. It will become as automatic as brushing your teeth. In fact, treat this book as your mental floss.

And, above all, have fun enhancing your communication skills. You'll soon notice how others struggle to compete with your new-found talent. You will discover a new 'you'. Subtle. Persuasive. Engaging. Confident. And you will relish every opportunity to try out your new skills.

Section One

Dump the Baggage
and Create Clarity

Chapter 1

Drop the Pink Elephant

*'I did **not** have sexual relations with that woman,*
Ms Lewinsky.'
US President Bill Clinton, January 1998

My friend Susan was lying in bed with the 'flu, barely able to move, but listening intently to ensure that her two-year-old next door was OK. The silence was unbearable. Susan sensed something was amiss. Finally, she had to find out.

'David,' she called out. Silence.
'David, are you being a good boy?' Silence, then a reply.
'I'm **not** eating my crayons, Mummy.'

Susan leapt out of bed and ran next door to find David, the carpet and the walls covered in half-chewed crayon.

Very young children make poor liars. They fail to recognize that an unprompted denial only prompts us to question the very thing they're denying. Once we grow up, we realize these things.

Or do we?

Let me quote Richard Nixon, President of the United States, in a televised address to the nation in April 1973: 'There can be **no** whitewash at the White House.' Until that point, the American people refused to believe that their president could have had any prior knowledge of the break-in at the Democratic Party HQ at the Watergate Building. That one phrase, linking the White House with a whitewash, reversed their thinking.

Surely a great communicator like President Bill Clinton would, 25 years later, avoid such a mistake. Surely a man whose every word has the power to change the world we live in ... surely a man whose every carefully-chosen utterance has been spun and re-spun by the world's finest spin doctors ... surely he would escape being so clumsy as to be 'caught short'? But we all remember the infamous 'I did **not** have sexual relations with that woman, Ms Lewinsky.' Ten months after making that televised statement, the President apologized for misleading the American people.

Try this one, then: 'I **didn't** stand on the radiator!'

This needs a little more explanation. I was in the kitchen of my home. A decorator was working away in my son's bedroom, when I heard a tremendous crash. Expecting to see an upturned ladder on top of the decorator, I was surprised and relieved to find them both upright. The radiator, however, was on its side and water was gushing in all directions.

Unprompted, the decorator opened up with 'I **didn't** stand on the radiator!'

Ladies and gentlemen of the jury, I put it to you that his denial was in fact an unintentional confession. Who suggested he had stood on it? Only the decorator himself!

Put together, all these denials have a common thread:

- 'I'm **not** eating my crayons.'

- 'There can be **no** whitewash at the White House.'

- 'I did **not** have sexual relations with that woman ...'

- 'I **didn't** stand on the radiator.'

In conclusion, m'lud:

1   Rather than being in direct reply to an accusation, these were all volunteered denials.

2   Notice how the words of denial – 'not', 'no', 'did not' and 'didn't' – are transparent. We automatically look through them for the real meaning.

3   They leave behind clear images: 'eating my crayons', 'whitewash at the White House', 'sexual relations with that woman' and 'stand on the radiator'.

This use of unprompted negatives is, to me, the biggest single flaw we demonstrate in our conversations. To make them easier to spot, I have given them a name. They are our Pink Elephants. Each one is highlighted in this book – along with the transparent denial – to help you spot them yourself in every conversation you ever have or hear.

If I said to you right now '**Don't** think of a Pink Elephant', the **don't** would disappear, leaving you with a clear picture of a Pink

Elephant. Similarly, if I said '**Don't** think of your boss naked', that would be the image that first came to mind.

So a Pink Elephant is an unnecessary, and normally vivid, negative. It usually pops up unprompted because it's part of the mental baggage we always carry around with us. If we're worried that somebody is thinking negatively about us, we say it before they do.

Pink Elephants are a great device for guarding against sloppy and ill-advised communication. I urge my clients to remember this key principle: always tell us what you are, instead of what you're not.

I ask them all to become Pink Elephant hunters.

The idea is to eliminate Pink Elephants altogether from your conversation, until you're Pink Elephant free. The whole process forces people to think and talk more positively. You see, speaking in negatives tells us very little. It often stops at the problem and fails to find the solution.

Alright, it's 9.50 p.m. You're on a dual carriageway, still a long way from home and in great need of a cup of coffee and a comfort stop. At last, a sign: 'Services. **Not** 24 hours.' **(Pink Elephant!)** Will they be open? Will they be closed? So what do you have to do? Slow down to see if the lights are on! That surely makes the case for a replacement sign reading 'Slow down to see if the lights are on.'

I was filming from a helicopter for a golf programme. The pilot was about to touch down when his colleague said on the radio

'That's **not** where you've to land.' **(Pink Elephant!)** Now hovering just 10 metres off the ground – more difficult than it looks – the pilot, somewhat exasperated, barked back 'Would you like to tell me where I should land, then?'

Some phrases you'll be all too familiar with in everyday conversation:

- 'I **don't** mean to be nosy, but …' **(Pink Elephant!)**

- 'I **don't** want to gossip, but …' **(Pink Elephant!)**

- 'I'm **not** trying to impose, but …' **(Pink Elephant!)**

- '**No** offence, but …' **(Pink Elephant!)**

- 'I **don't** mean to be rude, but …' **(Pink Elephant!)**

Remove the transparent denials and you're left with:

- 'I mean to be nosy …'

- 'I want to gossip …'

- 'I'm trying to impose …' And so on.

Pink Elephants only draw attention to the very thing you want to avoid.

This first came to my attention when reading an article about my appointment as BBC Scotland's sports reporter in 1986. The piece quoted me as saying my range of sporting interests would ensure that BBC Scotland was '**not** falling into the hole of only covering football'. **(Pink Elephant!)**

Was this some evil, twisted reporter in some scurrilous scandal sheet setting out to misquote me and make me look bad? No, this was an accurate piece, with an accurate quote in the BBC's own publication, the *Radio Times*. I had painted the very picture – 'falling into the hole of only covering football' – that I wanted to avoid. I had meant to say that I had covered 17 different sports that year alone.

Three conclusions struck me from what I had said that apply to us all:

1 We must take responsibility for the words we choose, whoever we're talking to.

2 We must put considerably more thought into our spoken words.

3 We must learn to DROP THE PINK ELEPHANT.

The thing was, I had been writing professionally since the age of 18 as a trainee newspaper reporter. By then in my late 20s, I had written for four newspapers, a radio station, Scottish Television and BBC TV news in Glasgow and London. I presented news and sport daily on the BBC. So was I really getting it wrong all the time?

The answer had to be a resounding 'yes'. It was masked by the fact that almost all my broadcast work was pre-written. It may have been spoken on air, but I had crafted it carefully beforehand and was reading from a script. And that's the situation we all face in comparing what we write in letters and reports with what we say on the phone and in face-to-face conversation. (I'll deal with lightning-fast and highly dangerous emails later.)

Most of us would check a letter for accuracy. We would possibly re-word a phrase that's woolly, tone down an inflammatory remark, show it to somebody else, chew it over and then send it. And what do we do in conversation? We speak, then we think, then we regret. And even that's only if we know what we've done wrong. But we're generally careless in conversation.

Most of us would benefit from spending less time worrying about what we guess others are thinking of us and more time telling them what we do believe in, what we have done, what we do stand for.

And, when an accusation is put to us, why repeat the allegation in the answer? If your partner asks if you're 'bored' with their news, why on earth would you want to tell them 'I'm **not** bored with your news'? **(Pink Elephant!)** That would only put the focus on 'bored'. Tell them instead you're keen to hear their news (providing you are, of course).

If your boss puts it to you that you 'lack ambition', tell him or her that you're 'highly ambitious' (provided you are). Every single Pink Elephant can be replaced with a positive.

It's all a question of agendas. Do you want to debate theirs or yours? If theirs is untrue, why waste your breath defending it? Tell them the truth instead. That applies equally whether you're speaking to a friend, relative, colleague or even a television reporter.

In one media training session I ran, a client unwittingly came out with 12 Pink Elephants in one three-minute interview. On analysing the interview, they divided roughly down the middle between negative words I had put into his mouth and negative words he had put into his own.

Start looking at your newspaper today and spot the Pink Elephant to find out what's really on someone's mind. Here's a selection to get you going. And remember to ignore the denial in bold letters to reveal the clear picture created. Because that's what your mind does.

Paul Burrell, former butler to Princess Diana, told us 'Telling my story was **never** about the money.' **(Pink Elephant!)** He went on to say the £300,000 deal with the *Daily Mirror* would pay off his debts. That strikes me as being about money.

A former Scotland captain's international football career came to an abrupt halt when he was banned after elbowing a San Marino player in the face. But instead of apologizing, Colin Hendry in one newspaper article told us, 'I **don't** do drugs. **(Pink Elephant!)** I **don't** drink and drive **(Pink Elephant!)** and I **don't** have five kids to three different women. **(Pink Elephant!)**'

In an attempt to pour cold water on newspaper stories that Stella McCartney was unhappy about the marriage of her dad,

Sir Paul, to former model Heather Mills, Stella's agent went public. But she only made matters worse: 'I'm **not** pretending that she's **never** exaggerated stories,' said Anya Noakes. **(Pink Elephant!)** 'But I **don't** think it's … been done with malicious intent.' **(Pink Elephant!)**

It can be highly amusing spotting other people's Pink Elephants, aware of what they really mean while they themselves are skirting round the issue. I witnessed one such incident at Faro airport in Portugal. A man in his early 20s was highly agitated as he joined a check-in queue. He needed to get back to Gatwick, but, as the conversation on his mobile unfolded, his frustration became obvious.

'Hi Ronnie, it's Jim. I'm stranded at Faro with precisely £15 in my pocket. I've been to the cash machine and the account's empty. How the **** am I meant to get back to Gatwick?' There was a short pause, followed by a classic Pink Elephant.

'Ronnie, I'm **not** blaming you!' **(Pink Elephant!)**
Another short pause, then:
'Well actually, Ronnie… I *am* blaming you!'
And that's what he had meant all along.

So, in order to improve your communication skills, you need to become a Pink Elephant hunter. This applies to your own communications as well as those of others. With a bit of application, you will take the first important steps to making Pink Elephants an endangered species.

Summary

1   Begin with some self-analysis. Are you using Pink Elephants?

2   Describe what is happening, rather than deny what you believe is someone else's perception of events. Stick to the positive point.

3   Hunt down the Pink Elephants in your conversations and those of others.

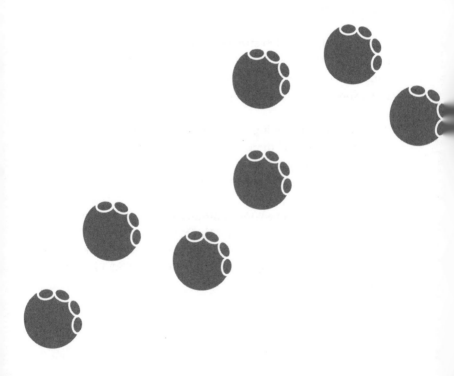

Chapter 2

Every Picture Tells a Story

'One small step for man. One giant leap for mankind.'
Neil Armstrong, on becoming the first man on the moon, July 1969

Now that you're hunting Pink Elephants, what else will paint a clearer picture of what you're saying?

Indulge me for a moment. Just think of the Eiffel Tower standing proud over the River Seine, dominating the Parisian skyline. Now recall the television news footage of a lone student standing up to an army tank in Tiananmen Square in Beijing, forcing the tank to move one way, then the other.

Now remember the shadowy but remarkable pictures of Neil Armstrong setting foot on the moon in July 1969, to the immortal words 'One small step for man. One giant leap for mankind.'

The better we can paint a picture of our thoughts with words, the more clearly we can see a picture.

It helps enormously if you've seen a picture of the Eiffel Tower or seen footage of the student and the tank or witnessed the moon landing. But the ability to paint the picture can take you beyond what you've already witnessed.

You could be in your garden or your car on a Sunday afternoon, listening to a radio commentator, who takes you to the 18th green of the final round of golf's Open Championship. 'So Tiger Woods squats down, adopting that familiar pose, cupping both hands around the brim of his cap, as he squints into the evening sunshine, reading the contours of this 15-foot downhill putt. He's over the ball. Fifteen feet between Tiger Woods and history. It's on its way towards the hole. Has he given it enough? Yes, he has!'

Without necessarily ever having seen the golf course in question, the image painted is sharp, clear and immediate. It's easy to see in your mind's eye. A carefully woven tapestry, building a bright, clear picture.

Most of us learned letters and then words in books by word–object association. 'A' is for apple and 'B' is for ball. Better still, give an object a name to make it really memorable, so 'F' is for 'Freddy the Fish'.

So when did we ever learn that 'S' is for structured finance or 'N' is for negative equity?

When I run seminars for tourism organizations, I point out that they start ahead of the game, because they can describe their products in the kind of imagery we see in brochures – castles, lakes or remote hotels in Highland glens.

By contrast, financial services are all about PEPs, ISAs, bonds and other abstracts that confuse us. The level of interpretation required is therefore higher and this is where so many people give up at the thought of such effort.

I was at a business lunch where each of us had three minutes to describe our enterprise to the other seven round the table. It so happened that I also had the 10-minute speaker's slot to address the 100 attendees of the lunch, so I told my table partners I would use my three minutes to speak about jargon.

As ever, I told my party piece about 'A' for apple and 'S' for structured finance. After I spoke, two others took their turn and then a man, who'd been sitting rather quietly, began cautiously.

'Well, I work in structured finance,' he began. 'Given what Bill's just said, I **don't** want to bore you about that. **(Pink Elephant!)** So I'll just stop there.' I laughed nervously, hoping that he was joking. But the stunned silence round the table suggested that he really had finished. My embarrassment was acute. I had made the crucial error of cracking a joke without first knowing who my audience was.

Fumbling, I turned reporter and asked the chap to explain structured finance, as I had always failed to grasp the concept. He had a couple of stabs. By now, we were all joining in with our questions. He did speak for three minutes but, after that time, I was still in the dark. Jargon led to jargon. Simple explanation was missing. I'm still unclear as to what structured finance is.

Now if you're in a position of leadership – boss, mother, father – you need to keep an eye on how well you jargon-bust.

I once asked a managing director if he was certain that every person in the room, including the newest recruits, would understand every word of his presentation. He replied 'Well, they should do. It's their job to keep up to speed.'

However he agreed, after further debate, that he would ensure his speech was jargon-free, therefore ensuring that every single word was understandable to every single person.

That's the trouble, you see. As you root out the jargon in your speech or presentation, you have to make the effort to convert it to plain English. And it takes considerable effort. So the onus for interpretation switches from the audience to you. That should be very welcome. It means that the audience will have a greatly-increased chance of following what you're saying.

How, then, do you identify what qualifies as jargon?

It's really very simple. If you were sitting in the audience with the knowledge of a new recruit – an absolute novice – would you understand every word? Before you answer that, can you remember being that new recruit?

In fact, we can make this simpler yet. Imagine you're in the audience, with little knowledge, expecting to be bored by the old bloke in the suit, droning on in jargon and TLAs ... sorry, Three Letter Acronyms (BBC, NHS, DSS). Now you've got the picture, make your speech the easiest one to understand that you've ever heard.

But what about the senior people in the organization? Surely this will be too simplistic for them? Well, it will be clear. It will be comprehensible. It will be constructed well. It will hold their attention because of its clarity. They'll mentally nod in agreement at the bits they already know and they'll learn from the bits they're hearing for the first time, or which they're even understanding for the first time.

And remember, you need to understand your message just as well as your audience. What could be worse than using jargon in the mistaken belief that everyone will know what you are talking about? But then you're challenged, only to reveal that you also are unable to explain what the jargon means.

It happened recently when a client, reading copy I had written for his organization, told his colleague that one sentence was guilty of 'bathos'. 'Bathos?' his colleague enquired. 'What on earth is that?'

The truth was that my client was unsure, and had to look it up in a dictionary, much to his discomfort. ('Bathos', I have now read, means 'unintentional anticlimax' – which is what the poor man suffered after his initially confident pronouncement.)

Some lawyers are still prone to using Latin as if it were English. I put this to one, who replied to our group 'I **don't** feel we use too much Latin *per se.'* **(Pink Elephant!)**

We all laughed – except him.

'What?' he demanded.
'Per se?' I explained.
'That's **not** really Latin,' he persisted. **(Pink Elephant!)**
'OK, what does it mean?' I asked.
'As such,' came the answer.
'What's wrong with just saying "as such",' I suggested, 'and saving us all reaching for the Latin dictionary?'

Language has become convoluted to avoid mistakes. It's defensive and vague to cover the options, especially in many businesses, where people are unsure of what they really mean. In my office, we joke that we're going to 'add value, going forward.' It now means nothing, because everybody in business is looking to 'add value, going forward.'

So why do we tolerate business jargon? To me, there's an element to this of the Hans Christian Andersen story of the Emperor's new clothes. Everybody was scared to tell the Emperor he was naked, so they praised him instead for his taste in new clothes.

Many people are scared to pipe up and say they're perplexed by the TLAs and mystified by other jargon. And who's going to tell the CEO – sorry, Chief Executive Officer – that 'adding value, going forward' is meaningless?

For that reason, the responsibility for eliminating jargon belongs to us all. If we want people to understand, we have to remove all jargon.

By contrast with all this mumbo-jumbo, the most inspirational speech I've ever heard was delivered by Frank Dick, British athletics coach to many of our successful Olympians of the mid-to-late 1980s.

He described people who lived in a valley, content with their warm, cosy if somewhat inward-looking life. He then described a villager who walked into the foothills and found the view interesting. He climbed higher and saw hills and valleys unseen by him before. The villager wondered if he had climbed high enough but, even though tired and cold, kept climbing.

And so his story went on until Frank asked the audience 'Do you want to be safe in the crowd, cloaked in the insularity of the valley? Or do you want to see how high you can climb in life? Do you want to go where your friend can only dream of going? Do you want to have the greatest view the world can offer you?'

I was mesmerized and told him so afterwards. His picture had transferred to my mind and, crucially, his concept (itself an abstract) was now firmly fixed in my thoughts. All by painting pictures with words.

Frank Dick was using mountain climbing as an analogy for achievement. He used a picture to replace the abstract, because abstracts are themselves most often invisible.

I find analogies incredibly powerful for that very reason. Suddenly a concept becomes clear. It makes sense.

A friend in financial services called me in to help him explain to his colleagues that their recent merger would be rough-going at first but would be hugely beneficial in the long term. I said I would give it some thought.

'It's like two large rivers coming together,' I suggested, after a few minutes. 'Both are coming from different directions and so, when they meet, there is enormous turbulence. But a little further downstream, this one great river has harnessed the power of that turbulence and it's all flowing much more smoothly, yet still powerfully. All the water's moving in the same direction.' Doug liked it and used it. The picture helped his team envisage a more certain future.

My younger daughter, Emma, was upset when I started working two days a week on BBC's *Breakfast News* programme in London. This required me to leave my Glasgow home each Sunday night and return from London on the Tuesday. Emma thought this was a bad idea and demanded to know why I was leaving her two days most weeks.

Had I forgotten her age, I would have told her that the presentation experience was invaluable and the profile indispensable, as it increased my worth in the corporate sector, adding to the Broadcasting Business's bottom line. Thankfully, I remembered that she was five and so told her that every time I went to London, the BBC paid me money. And when we had enough in the bank, we'd go to see Mickey Mouse in Florida.

In a flash, she was handing me my briefcase, opening the door and waving goodbye.

Now it would be rather patronizing to speak to adults in that fashion, because the message would be pitched well below their level of understanding. But it's essential with any audience to find the language they understand, pitch the message at their level and give them time to digest it.

If you can find an analogy appropriate to the audience, you are on to a winner.

So, when using analogies, find appropriate ones that *everyone* can relate to. And work them to a conclusion BEFORE you have to use them for real.

On one occasion, a client sweetly simplified the subject matter of an interview by explaining 'effluent' in plain English. 'Effluent', she began, 'is, for example, what you're left with in a pot when you've boiled and removed the potatoes.'

'Brilliantly simple,' I enthused. 'I can see what you're talking about and understand clearly what you mean.' We looked forward to her colleague repeating the explanation in her interview. However, a little flustered, she got mixed up with her untried analogy and blurted 'Effluent's just like scum in a pot.'

Right idea, wrong form of words.

So remember, try out those analogies before you use them in earnest.

Summary

1   Speak in vivid pictures to paint clear descriptions.

2   Use analogies to turn abstract concepts and jargon into bright pictures.

3   Avoid talking above or below your audience's level. Instead, talk to their level.

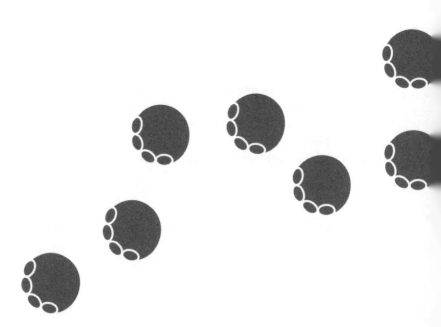

Section Two

Be Principled in What You Say

Chapter 3

Staying on the Louisiana Highway

*'The sooner you're replaced by a machine,
the better for all of us.'*
Bill McFarlan, November 1993

It was late evening on a wet and windy November day when I arrived back at Glasgow Airport. I had been up since 4.30 a.m. to present sports bulletins on the BBC's *Breakfast News* programme and then run a media training course at the London headquarters of Guinness.

The journey to Heathrow Airport had been fraught and the flight was delayed. I was now exhausted, having used all my energy first to present sport and then cajole and encourage my course participants. In short, I was fresh out of what I call 'professional politeness'. Anybody coming between a soothing bath and me was likely to pay the price. However, in 30 minutes I would be in the sanctuary of my home, able to relax. I had only to find my car, pay for the parking ticket and drive home.

The car was at the far end of the car park, so I was soaked as I reached it. Approaching the tollbooth, I placed the ticket between my teeth and fumbled in my pocket for a ten pound note. With rain lashing down, I reluctantly opened the window and placed the note on the narrow ledge of the booth… only for a gust of wind to blow it inside.

'There's **no** need to throw it at me,' snapped the officious woman in the booth. **(Pink Elephant!)**
'I did**n't** throw it at you. **(Pink Elephant!)** It was the wind,' I sighed.
'And I **don't** want your half-chewed ticket either,' she snarled. **(Pink Elephant!)**
'Well it's **not** as if I have AIDS,' I hissed. **(Pink Elephant!)**
'You might for all I know,' she spat back.
That was it. I lost all composure.
'The sooner you're replaced by a machine, the better for all of us,' I barked. 'Have a happy redundancy.'

I snatched my change and screeched off feeling pretty good about my parting shot. I had shown her. How dare she treat her customer that way! Had she any idea how hard I had worked that day and how tired I was?

On relating the story at home, I now found it rather funny. Although, judging by the open-jawed expressions around the kitchen table, my family seemed to be missing the humour.

A week later, returning from my next stint at *Breakfast News*, it was mid-afternoon and the sun was shining. I was positively happy until a sense of foreboding began to suffocate me. What if the same woman was on duty at the pay booth and remembered me?

The smugness of seven days earlier had turned to guilt, although I was attempting to bury it in self-justification. In reality, I was now regretting my outburst. Despite her sniping, the machine gun fire

I had released was unjustifiable. An escalation of the spat would have been avoidable, had I only shown one ounce of humility.

The trouble was my tiredness, and my resulting lack of professional politeness. But, at that time of night, I bet she was tired as well. I had been presenting a television programme and teaching media handling skills while she had been stuck in a cold and draughty booth, taking grief from ticket-sucking, wet, tired and grumpy customers like me. For all I knew, she may even have been told that day that she *was* to be replaced by a machine.

If I had only met her 'no need to throw it at me' comment with 'I'm sorry, the wind caught it', I'm sure we could have left on good terms.

What would I have done with a client? Remained polite throughout, of course. Shame on you Bill – you hypocrite!

Some years later, at the same airport – and after another long day in London – I was queuing at the machine to stamp my parking ticket. (The pay booths had been replaced but, ironically, one of the few people to keep their jobs in a customer care centre was my friend, the former collector of soggy, disease-ridden tickets.)

Just as it was my turn at the machine, I dropped a couple of pound coins on the floor. Scrambling to pick them up, I noticed people behind me in the queue edging forward towards the machine.

'I think you'll find there's a queue,' I announced, in best Basil Fawlty style.

'Oh Bill, it's yourself,' came the reply, to my horror. 'Remember you ran a training course for us in London last month?'

Suddenly, I was all charm. All professional politeness. All embarrassment.

So at what point do you learn to engage the brain before putting the mouth in gear? Normally when your logic kicks in before an emotional response to your ego coming under attack.

These two incidents taught me a valuable lesson. I now have a technique in place that helps me stay cool. It involves 'remaining on the Louisiana Highway, rather than straying into the swamp'. Put simply, it's about keeping to the moral high ground in any argument.

Keeping to the highway may well start off by offering the other person a get-out clause, avoiding a tricky situation. One such situation arose when I found a woman sitting on my seat on a plane.

I looked at my boarding pass. It was 10C. I checked the seat she occupied. It was 10C. Now I've misread both the boarding pass and the seat number in the past, so I checked again.

Then I began. 'Excuse me, I wonder if I have the right boarding pass.'

'10C,' she said, looking at my pass, before repeating the number and looking above her head. She then rifled through her bag to find her own pass, numbered 9C. 'Oh I'm sorry,' she said.

'It's quite all right,' I replied. 'I find the numbering slightly confusing.'

Painless! I got my seat. She got hers. We avoided a needless confrontation.

However, I once witnessed a similar situation involving two women go horribly wrong. One strode up the passageway, clearly harassed, and announced to the other 'I think you'll find you're in my seat. 15A.'

The seated woman remained cool, checked her own boarding pass, then asked to see the other passenger's card. 'Well, I would be,' she then replied, 'if I were going to Amsterdam. But I'm going to Heathrow … along with everyone else.'

Nonchalantly, she resumed reading her newspaper as the aggressor marched back down the passageway, bleeding from self-inflicted wounds. She was accompanied off the plane by much pointing and sniggering from other passengers.

To claim the moral high ground – and stay on the Louisiana Highway – all you have to do is remain polite and reasonable. Even if you get off on the wrong foot, you can always retrieve the situation and still come up smelling of roses.

I was enjoying a weekend in the south-west of England with my wife and another couple. Ready to go out for dinner, Caroline and I arrived in the bar before the others came down. I went to the counter to order. Fifteen minutes later, our friends were still absent, so I went up for another round.

When I returned with the drinks, I looked at my change and realized I had been overcharged. The barman was busy when I arrived back, so my argument was well-prepared. Firmly, but politely, I told him he had made a mistake and charged me £1.25 more for exactly the same drinks as before.

Triumphantly, I sat down, my money returned. At which point, Caroline pointed out that my arithmetic was wrong. The difference in price was only 25 pence. After several more checks, I reluctantly agreed.

'But I've still been overcharged by 25p,' I insisted to her.

'Yes, it was 25 pence more,' she pointed out. 'But I had a gin and bitter lemon this time. It was a gin and tonic last time. That would account for it.'

Yes, yes, yes ... and yes again. The barman was right. I was wrong, wrong, wrong! So what now? Time to deal with the unpalatable truth. I lifted the £1.25 and went back to the bar to apologize to a now-baffled barman.

'I'm very sorry,' I began, 'the mistake was all mine.'

Now totally bemused, he took my money and got on with his increasingly confusing duties. I returned to my seat feeling foolish, but now guilt-free.

The 30-second apology turned out to be a wise investment of my time. The barman, it turned out, also served at breakfast, where I bade him 'good morning'. He helped us downstairs with our luggage, then he checked us out of the hotel. It seemed that some greater force was telling him to shadow me, to ensure I remained humble. If so, the trick worked. I crept out the hotel with my case under one arm and my humility under the other.

Summary

1   *Retain the moral high ground by remaining patient and polite.*

2   *Be sure of your facts and use only polite explanation.*

3   *That's how to stay on the Louisiana Highway, rather than getting stuck in the swamp.*

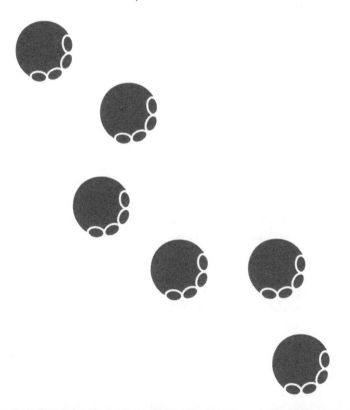

Chapter 4

Sorry Seems to be the Hardest Word

'Any fool can defend his mistake – and most fools do.'
Dale Carnegie, *How to Win Friends and Influence People*

Elton John was spot-on when he sang 'Sorry Seems to be the Hardest Word'.

To be wrong hurts us deeply. It shakes our self-confidence. It makes us doubt our ability. But the truth may well be that we simply got it wrong.

Is it possible to go through your whole life being right all the time? Some people would certainly give you the impression that they, or their organization, are infallible.

Most of us hate having to say 'I'm sorry, I got it wrong'. I reckon that's because our self-confidence is a little more fragile than we would like others to believe. But the quicker we come to realize our mistakes, and the quicker we apologize, the quicker the growing tension evaporates.

Refusal to apologize increases the tension – and increases the mistrust of the judgement of the person in the wrong. Refusal to apologize leads to wrongful imprisonment, huge compensation claims, even wars.

Caroline jokes (at least I hope she's joking) that the first time she heard me apologize was when I got a football scoreline wrong on television. I used that anecdote when calming down a potentially explosive situation at the Women's World Doubles Tennis Championship final in Edinburgh a few years ago, in my role as Master of Ceremonies.

From our office above the grandstand, Gavin, the tournament organizer, and I looked out in puzzlement at the quarter-full stadium as the final got underway at one o'clock on the dot. 'I'm at a loss!' he exclaimed. 'Where is everybody? We're sold out.'

Then the penny dropped. The tickets were advertising a 1.30 p.m. start, but a late decision by the BBC to televise the event meant the start time had been brought forward by half an hour.

Gavin was distraught. So, too, were the fans gathering round the stewards, who were preventing ticket holders from taking their seat because play had started. Their anger was growing at the suggestion that they should have been in their seats in time for the start of play. 'What on earth are we going to do?' Gavin asked, to nobody in particular.

'Well, as Master of Ceremonies, I reckon it's my job to go on court at the end of the first set and apologize,' I suggested.

'But that will make things worse,' he replied. 'People will demand their money back. The papers will be full of complaints.'

'Only if we do nothing,' I offered. 'Trust me.'

He did and, amid rumbles of discontent, I strode out on court at the set break, with a final instruction ringing in my ears: **'Don't blame the BBC!' (Pink Elephant!)**

'Trust me,' I replied.

As the players wiped their brows and their racquets, I was the one having to face the heat.

'Ladies and Gentlemen,' I began. 'We owe you an explanation and an apology. You turned up on time for a 1.30 start, but we've published the wrong start time. The ticket should have said 1 o'clock. Now I can only apologize for that. We've had a great first set of tennis and I'm looking forward to some more enthralling play, this time with everybody seated. Again, please accept our apologies – and enjoy the match.'

The end of the announcement was marked with a faint ripple of half-hearted applause. But the match stretched to three sets and the crowd loved it. The stewards reported to us that the only complaints they received came before the announcement.

'How did you know that would work?' Gavin asked.

'They only wanted to know the mistake was ours and that they were right to arrive when they did,' I replied. The apology was simply asking them to forgive our mistake, which they did. Their self-confidence was intact. Ours was dented.

Gavin was astonished. But then, he was more emotionally involved than me. I may have been the frontman, but the mistake was his. And I found it much easier to apologize for his mistake than I would have had it been mine.

Some years later, I was attempting to record a weekly football show I presented for Sky Television. A new graphics operator was struggling with 'finger trouble' – pressing the wrong buttons, leaving captions to appear at all the wrong times. What should have taken 45 minutes took twice as long. Every time he made another mistake, we had to return to the previous edit point and start again.

Everybody was frustrated and I was starting to lose concentration. The longer this went on, the more I began to stumble, meaning we had to go back to the last edit point, only this time because of me.

After two hours, the producer, director and I emerged from the studio frazzled. But, by now, the blame fell on the shoulders of the graphics operator AND me. After all, I had contributed to the length of the recording. There was only one thing to do. 'I'm really sorry about the stumbles,' I offered. 'I started to lose concentration.'

They almost fell over themselves to let me off the hook. 'It's **not** your fault,' the producer said. **(Pink Elephant!)** 'Anybody would have lost the plot,' added the director.

Had I chosen to blame the poor graphics man, both would have been justified in pointing out my shortcomings. I had simply empowered them to accept my apology. We all benefited from that.

The trouble is, many organizations see it differently. They believe, wrongly in my view, that to say 'sorry' is to admit weakness. I believe the opposite. I believe it's a sign of strength. We all make mistakes. Why deny that? But those who claim infallibility usually fall in the estimation of people more realistic than themselves.

We've seen governments, churches, courts and police forces fail to apologize when they've clearly got it wrong.

Anyone who has followed the tragic story of four suspicious deaths at the Deepcut Army Barracks in Surrey would see why an apparent lack of sympathy creates deep-felt anger.

Four young soldiers, three men and a woman, have been found dead there with gunshot wounds in recent years. The Army says they are all suicides, even though one soldier suffered two head wounds (from above) and another soldier suffered FIVE chest wounds.

Parents of the young soldiers reported a dismissive attitude shown by the Army.

When phoning three days after his son's death to hear how the enquiry was going, Jim Collinson reports being told 'There was one body, one gun. Draw your own conclusions.' That attitude has only provoked the parents into pursuing the matter as far as it takes to seek justice.

Meanwhile a Ministry of Defence (MOD) spokeswoman gave her feelings away with a string of denials:

- 'We have **nothing** to cover up ...' **(Pink Elephant!)**

- '... **nothing** to hide ...' **(Pink Elephant!)**

- 'It would be foolish to say bullying and harassment **doesn't** happen.' **(Pink Elephant!)**

When a Chinook helicopter crashed into the Mull of Kintyre in south-west Scotland in June 1994, killing 29 – among them many senior intelligence figures from the armed forces – the MOD put it down to 'gross (pilot) negligence with absolutely **no** doubt whatsoever.' **(Pink Elephant!)**

The pilots' parents, and a growing number of people showing interest in the case, disagreed. A House of Lords committee concluded in February 2002 that technical problems related to computer software were the most likely cause of the crash. The House of Lords report exonerated the two pilots. The Ministry has yet to apologize. Indeed, a spokeswoman stated 'We stand by the conclusions of the (MOD) enquiry and review officers.'

Recent history in Britain is peppered with people who have been wrongfully imprisoned, among them the Guildford Four (15 years in prison), the Birmingham Six (16 years in prison) and the Bridgewater Three (over 17 years in prison). Their fight for justice was fuelled by the intransigence of the authorities.

Stefan Kiszko, a man of limited intelligence, was jailed in 1976 for a child murder despite forensic tests which, had they been shared with the court at the time, would have proved him innocent. He was released 16 years later in 1992 and died within six months, without ever hearing an apology from anybody in authority.

More recently in 2002, Robert Brown – jailed for murder in 1977 when aged just 19 – was freed at the age of 45 after his murder conviction was quashed. Corruption among police officers involved in his conviction had first come to light when one of them was jailed in 1983.

People in high places who make big mistakes seldom apologize.

Shirley McKie was a Strathclyde Police detective sent to investigate a murder. She was accused of leaving her fingerprint on a doorway above the body, having been told specifically to keep out of the building. When she refused to admit in the witness box at the murder trial that the print was hers, she was charged with perjury and was herself sent for trial for lying under oath.

In a celebrated case, she became the first person in 102 years of Scottish fingerprint evidence to prove a positive fingerprint identification to be wrong. She won the court case, was commended by the judge and subsequently received an apology from the Scottish Justice Minister in Parliament. Seven years later, she had still to receive an apology from any of her accusers – and so successfully sued her former employers.

'I would still be working for the police today if they had just said "sorry, we got it wrong",' Shirley told me. 'Instead, I was dragged through court, my career is over and the taxpayer has paid out millions of pounds to fund this charade. All because of a refusal to say "sorry".'

Many lawyers used to advise that saying 'sorry' would cost money. The opposite is often the case. Saying it at the earliest opportunity will often prevent legal action.

There are occasions when you can acknowledge someone's anger and distress, even when you feel liability lies elsewhere. 'I'm sorry you're upset,' is the very recognition some people seek. Even the sharpest lawyer would have to concede that liability is unaffected by that sort of apology. You could say 'I'm sorry that the Twin Towers tragedy ever happened.' But the responsibility for it happening lies elsewhere.

Things are changing. There is a greater recognition than there used to be when something goes wrong that putting it right starts with an apology. In the two decades I've been advising companies on handling the media, this is one of the most encouraging changes I've witnessed.

Any time the world's biggest alcoholic drinks company, Diageo, has announced redundancies, it has apologized for having to do so. When BP at Grangemouth announced 700 job losses in November 2001, it prefaced the announcement by expressing its regrets. All my other clients take the same view.

As more and more companies realize that their reputation is linked to community relations, environmental responsibility and also share price, the growing tendency to put up a corporate hand in apology becomes increasingly accepted as the right thing to do.

My strong feeling is that any declining confidence in the police, the courts and government would be addressed by more frequent apologies when things go wrong.

Regret, Reason and Remedy

So we can accept that it's often right to apologize. Is that enough? Certainly not! How are you going to fix what you've got wrong?

There is a simple formula to remember when all your emotions are telling you to run for cover and hide. It's called Regret, Reason and Remedy – the Three Rs.

Two tragic air disasters in Britain within 18 days of each other in the late 1980s contrasted the attitudes of the airlines involved. One applied the Three Rs, the other was posted missing.

The bombing of Pan Am's transatlantic flight, a couple of days before Christmas 1988, ripped the heart out of Lockerbie and was a shocking catastrophe that caught the world's attention. Pan Am must have been stunned at what happened to their aircraft and that may be why they failed to appear at the crash site to tell the world how they felt about the biggest mass murder in British history.

The British Midland crash at Kegworth on the M1 motorway happened on 8 January 1989 after the engine of a Belfast-bound plane from Heathrow caught fire. The 47 deaths were a personal tragedy for all those involved, including Chairman Sir Michael Bishop, witnessing loss of life on one of his aircraft for the first time. I vividly recall him at the crash scene that night, engulfed by news cameras. He looked a distraught figure, attempting to absorb what had happened to his aircraft and his passengers. In each interview he expressed the grief he was feeling (Regret), explained that an investigation was underway to find the cause

(Reason) and promised that any changes that could be made in the future would be made (Remedy).

Several years later, I met Sir Michael at a function and told him how much I had empathized with him that awful night and admired his handling of the disaster. 'I was fortunate to be half an hour away at the time of the crash,' he said. 'What if the accident had happened in the South of France?'

'I reckon you'd have been in the South of France just as soon as a plane could take you,' I answered. 'It was the attitude that shone through that night. Where you had happened to be at the time was irrelevant.'

Ironically, while terrorism was the cause of the Lockerbie disaster, fire and pilot error led to the Kegworth crash. Yet it was Pan Am who were noticeable by their absence, while British Midland stood up to face the music, to their great credit.

Three years after Lockerbie, Pan Am folded, bringing to an end 64 years of pioneering aviation. From operating its first flight in 1927, a single-engine aircraft route between Key West in Florida and Havana in Cuba, Pan Am had become industry leaders. But the company's handling of the Lockerbie aftermath indicated that something was very wrong with their public face.

British Midland has gone from strength to strength, despite taking the blame over the cause of the Kegworth crash and the 47 deaths that resulted from it.

Regret, Reason and Remedy apply to any situation, business or domestic, that goes wrong.

I received a phone call from a client in the energy industry one sunny Saturday morning as I was out and about in the car. In a week when there had already been a loss of power and a small explosion at his plant, my client now had a fire to deal with. He was looking for my advice in dealing with the media. I reminded him of Regret, Reason and Remedy, which then gave him a structure to build on for his newspaper, radio and television interviews that day.

Firstly, he had to apologize to the local community for the noise and smoke pouring out of the plant (Regret). Then he had to explain what had happened to start the fire, and that it had been tackled successfully (Reason). Finally, he had to explain how long it would be until things were back to normal – and what would be done to prevent a recurrence of the problem (Remedy). He agreed that this was the way to handle it and carried out his task well throughout the day.

The Three Rs are applicable in all sorts of circumstances, if used sincerely. And of course it's important that you really do everything in your power to prevent recurrence.

Use the Three Rs when running late for a meeting. You probably hate being late and feel you want to apologize all day for your seemingly inexcusable mistake. But that's all baggage. So remember to get things in perspective by using the Three Rs – and to progress beyond just the apology:

- 'I'm really sorry I'm late. (Regret)

- I misjudged the traffic this morning and got held up in a jam. (Reason)

- If you like, I'll shorten the lunch break to ensure we finish on time.' (Remedy)

Going back to the starting time cock-up at the tennis tournament, that was classic Three Rs:

- 'I'm sorry we got it wrong.

- We printed the wrong start time.

- We'll now get underway with everybody seated (and pray for a long match).'

You'll often feel that situations are made worse by people telling you what's wrong but omitting either to apologize or solve the problem. In other words, Reason – without the Regret and Remedy!

Recently I watched a young member of staff at a leisure club struggle through a morning in which the swimming pool had run out of towels. She met every member with the same message: 'There are **no** towels!' **(Pink Elephant!)** This, of course, was the problem. What was the solution? Regret and Remedy were both missing.

I wrote out the three Rs on a piece of paper and said to her to try this:

- 'I'm sorry we're out of towels this morning. (Regret)

- We've been let down by the delivery company. (Reason)

- They've promised to deliver fresh towels by 10 a.m., so can I ask you to use your own in the meantime?' (Remedy)

Of course sometimes it's impossible to predict exactly when a problem will be solved. And pointing out that it's difficult to make a prediction is infinitely preferable to hazarding a guess that turns out to be wrong.

The power company 24seven failed to live up to its name when 300,000 of their three million customers in southern and eastern England were left without electricity following gales in the autumn of 2002, some of them for eight days. A string of dissatisfied customers reported through the media how answering-machine messages had assured them daily that they would be reconnected that day – only to miss the target time and time again. Every missed deadline brought a fresh outcry.

One winter, another major power supplier in Britain suffered loss of supply over a large area of the countryside, after snow brought down power lines. In an effort to ease the discontent of customers, they gave assurances that power would be restored within 24 hours, then 48 hours, then 72 hours.

Each deadline was missed for legitimate reasons. Conditions and damage were worse than first thought.

When a similar snowfall inflicted severe damage several years later, the power company resisted media demands for a timetable for restoration of supply. They expressed regret at the loss of power, explained that snow had brought down remote lines and said that they were working flat out in freezing conditions to repair the damage and restore power.

It was impossible to say when that would happen, they pointed out, because the extent of the damage was still unknown. This time, the reaction from customers was much more positive.

It was a lesson in managing expectations.

Summary

1   *Saying 'sorry' is the best way to start rebuilding confidence in your relationship after something has gone wrong.*

2   *We respect those who apologize – and lose respect for those who pretend to be infallible.*

3   *Regret, Reason and Remedy offers an apology, explanation and solution. It manages expectation, which must then be met.*

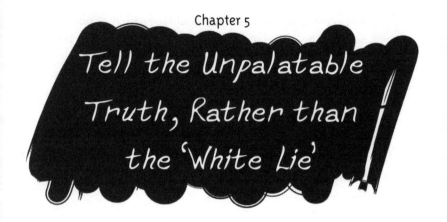

Chapter 5

Tell the Unpalatable Truth, Rather than the 'White Lie'

'If you tell the truth, you don't have to remember anything.'
Mark Twain

So first of all, how do you define the truth? Would that be the unshakable, undeniable, unquestionable truth – or simply the truth as you see it?

Going on the basis that facts are truths, I asked a group of business leaders to tell me two facts from the Lockerbie Trial, in which two Libyan citizens were accused of bombing a Pan Am flight, resulting in the deaths of 270 people.

'One man was guilty, one was innocent,' came a quick reply, referring to the verdict of a Scottish court, convened in the The Hague.
'No, that's an opinion,' I replied.
'Well the court found one man guilty,' came the redrafted reply.

'Correct. The court found him guilty. And whose decision was that?' I asked.

'Three independent Scottish judges,' came the reply.

'Who says they were independent?' I again teased. 'I thought they were paid by the Scottish Judiciary.'

'All right, three judges appointed by the Scottish courts.'

'Correct,' I replied. 'Now we're getting to the truth and away from opinions.'

We read, hear and see opinions every day, wrapped up as facts, often because the speaker sees that opinion as the truth, sometimes because it suits their agenda.

I was overseas when the trial of Barry George – accused of murdering TV presenter Jill Dando – came to an end. The only newspaper I could find was the *Daily Express* which used half its front page to reproduce just one word: GUILTY.

I must declare that I wanted Barry George to be guilty. Having very fond memories of co-presenting with Jill on *Breakfast News* for three years, I wanted the right person to be caught, tried and put out of harm's way. However, deep down I have to accept that 'guilty' is only an opinion, rather than a fact.

It was the opinion of ten jurors (one disagreed and one was discharged) that Barry George killed Jill Dando. And in the absence of Barry George admitting the crime (and of that confession being the truth), 'guilty' will remain an opinion.

A course participant vigorously disagreed with this point recently. His argument was that we must accept a court's decision to be the truth. I asked him why on earth we would want to do that. It can only ever be an opinion. Isn't that what jurors are asked to do: give their opinion?

Sometimes the truth can only be defined by how far we're willing to go to establish the facts.

Our lives are bombarded with opinions from those with points to score, money to make and axes to grind. Politicians offer us opinions, advertisers offer us opinions, businesses offer us opinions – all dressed as facts.

Are they the only offenders? Of course not – we're all at it!

- 'The service here is shocking.' Opinion.

- 'There's little worth watching on TV tonight.' Opinion.

- 'He's always late.' Opinion.

- 'That company's useless.' Opinion.

The only way these opinions can be redeemed as facts is to add a phrase like 'in my opinion' or 'from my point of view'

One of the first things I learned in journalism was to be cautious over what's opinion and what's fact. 'The red BMW crashed into the white Ford van' is an opinion that may well be challenged in court. 'The red BMW and white Ford van were in collision' is a fact. Good journalism adheres to the old adage 'If in doubt, leave it out.' Bad journalism often chooses to ignore it.

So how do you ensure you're telling the truth, rather than merely spouting opinions when talking to people? Certainly, by personalizing what you're saying: 'I really feel the service here is shocking … there's little of interest to me on TV tonight … it seems to me he's always late …' and 'I find that company useless.'

There are two other issues that stand in the way of the truth here. Firstly, many are concerned that, by giving only part of the story, we're fudging the truth. In my view, we're highly selective in the way we present our opinions. We most often choose only that part of the argument or story that suits our case.

People with a scientific background – doctors, engineers, physicists, chemists, architects – often tell me they feel unable to do justice to a subject they've been asked to explain briefly. Their scientific minds worry that huge chunks are left out.

In reality, most people want the news headlines rather than the correspondent's 30-minute report. So being succinct will inevitably mean leaving bits out. It's then just a case of attempting to be balanced. But, as we've seen earlier, we should all be remembering to keep it simple and talk in pictures.

So that's the first issue standing in the way of the truth. The second is more obvious. People lie.

They lie about their weight, their age, their motives, why they were late, what they think of your clothes, what they think of your best friend. Discretion is often the better part of valour. Is it wise when your partner asks 'Have I put on a pound or two?' to answer 'At a conservative estimate …'? Of course not!

But I'm talking about the 'white lie', told to make up for your own failings because 'it does **no** harm'. **(Pink Elephant!)**

I disagree entirely. It does enormous harm.

If you told a friend or colleague you were late because your car broke down, only for him to discover you were late because you set out on the journey impossibly late, he would grow suspicious of your motives and question your trustworthiness.

Why did you lie? Were you unable to confront the truth, or is there another reason? Why not just apologize, admit that you left too late and suggest you go straight out and skip the coffee? In other words, Regret, Reason and Remedy.

Let me contrast two events at our home in the same summer.

The first was the infamous incident involving the decorator, the broken-and-now-gushing radiator and the Pink Elephant. 'I **didn't** stand on the radiator,' was his first utterance. (Did I say he had?)

This massive Pink Elephant was the first in a series of lies he told me, leading me to pursue him for half the cost of the extensive plumbing bill to put right the damage.

Contrast this with the handyman painting the eaves at the front of the house, some 30 feet up. From my basement office, I could hear a crashing sound, followed, a minute later, by a more tentative knock on the office door.

Ashen-faced and paint-splattered, Peter was about to make a confession. 'I'm really sorry,' he began. 'I was right up at the eaves when I dropped the full bucket of white paint. It's gone all over your steps. Do you by any chance have any turps and some cloths so I can clean it up?'

Regret, Reason, Remedy.

It would have been difficult to blame divine intervention or some other reason for the paint falling to earth. But his immediate confession of the unpalatable truth with an apology, explanation and action plan made me sympathetic. I even admired his courage and honesty as I watched a river of white gloss paint imitate Niagara Falls right down my front steps.

Interestingly, when I met Peter at a party years later, I knew his face was familiar – although this time unsplattered. It was he who caught my eye and exclaimed 'Oh, the steps!' I had actually forgotten it was he who dropped the paint bucket.

Had he opted for the 'white lie' – and it would have been a gloss white lie – at the time, the sight of him would have annoyed me and should have left him embarrassed to meet me again.

As it was, we laughed about the incident – because things do go wrong and it's how you handle them that matters.

One final point: the truth is easier to remember because it happened. Lies are figments of the imagination. As such, they're easier to forget.

Summary

1   The truth can be defined by how far you're willing to go to establish a fact.

2   The truth is reality, while a lie is a figment of the imagination.

3   Once a lie is discovered, you're a liar.

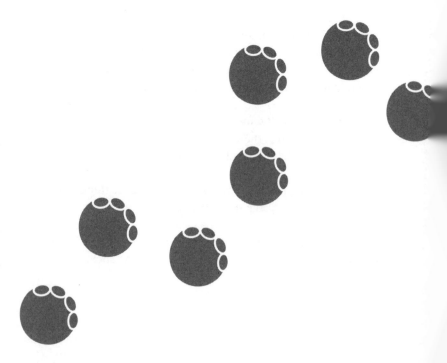

Chapter 6

Thank You and Well Done

'Well done is better than well said.'
Benjamin Franklin

It was almost midnight in the northern Spanish town of San Sebastian. Along with the entire production crew, I had been working since 7 a.m., filming the annual BBC contest, *World's Strongest Man*.

We were all shattered but, despite the usual setbacks, filming had gone well. The last event of the day, set in an open-air restaurant, had finished barely ten minutes before and we were all now ready for a drink at the bar.

Typically, the producer, Simon Betts, was first to put his hand in his pocket. As he thrust a cool beer in my hand, he began: 'Master,' (he called all the men 'Master') 'that was a great day's work. Your scripts were well written. The pieces to camera were bright and enthusiastic and the commentary was sharp and on the ball. Well done!'

I felt like a million dollars. This was my first big presentation job for a BBC UK-wide audience. The show would be shown across the BBC network on Boxing Day to an audience of over 13 million and syndicated across the world. Frankly, I would have done it for nothing, but I was being well paid for the privilege.

My confidence was at an all-time high. And yet I had always given the job in hand my best shot. So what was so good this time? Quite simply, Simon Betts was the first producer/editor/chief reporter ever to detail what he liked about my work. Indeed, as far as I could recall, he was the first person in my 14 years in newspapers, radio and television to thank me for my day's work.

Now, I'll ask you this question: how often are you thanked warmly – and at length – for a good day's work or giving a helping hand? Or how often do you thank your staff, colleagues, family or friends with the depth of praise that their efforts deserve? I would predict that the answer to both would be 'less often than is deserved'.

Some years after San Sebastian, I was running a presentation skills training course for a very senior manager in the financial services sector. We got on to the subject of motivation and I recalled the story of Simon Betts. She seemed rather indifferent to what I had just said, so I asked what she said to her staff as they were leaving the office at night. 'I ask them what they've contributed to the business that day,' she replied.

There was an awkward pause as I scrambled for the right response to what she had said. All I could do was feebly repeat her answer, which she then confirmed. I then asked what impact she thought that would have on her colleagues.

'It will make them think more deeply about what they should be doing,' she replied.

'Or it will make them question why they bothered working hard that day if their efforts went unrecognised,' I suggested.

I often wonder what she says to her staff these days – and if anybody enjoys working for her.

I had the pleasure of working with Simon Betts on two further productions of *World's Strongest Man*. These three seven-day shoots were among the most arduous pieces of work I've ever undertaken.

We were at breakfast generally between six and seven each morning and we often worked until ten or eleven in the evening. After San Sebastian, the following year's programme was shot in Finland in a heat wave and my final programme was recorded in Tenerife at the height of a Canaries summer. But while the shops and bars of Tenerife closed each day for the siesta, the BBC crew worked on.

Simon kept us going through the heat of the afternoon. He was extremely particular. If dissatisfied with a piece-to-camera or certain shot, he would call for a retake. Again and again until he was satisfied we'd got it right.

But he had our respect. Indeed, I felt he could have presented the programme better than I could. He had been a floor manager with BBC TV's *Morecambe and Wise Show* in the 70s, generally regarded as the best light entertainment programme of its kind.

In short, Simon knew exactly what he wanted and, more importantly, how to get it from his team.

His compliments, however, posed me a problem. Because this kind of praise was new to me, I was awkward in accepting it. I would normally mumble a reply that suggested I was undeserving of the praise and that he had the harder task as producer/director.

Yet the cameraman, who had worked with Simon many times before, would simply reply 'Thanks Simon. My pleasure. You did a great job yourself.' Simple really.

On reflection, I realized that Simon would prefer that I accept his praise, rather than reject it. It's like handing someone a bunch of flowers you've chosen specially for them, only for them to say 'no thanks'.

So I resolved to work harder at accepting praise.

Most Americans do it effortlessly. We have an American friend, born and raised in South Carolina, where politeness abounds. At Elizabeth's wedding in Charleston, I watched this beautiful bride being lavished with compliments on her appearance, her choice of husband ... everything. She could have self-consciously rejected each compliment, causing unease among her guests. Instead, she did what comes naturally, replying 'Why, thank you,' to each and every praise-laden remark. And she meant it.

By year three of *World's Strongest Man*, I had learned much from the manner of Simon Betts. The crew was remarking on the last night that the hotel had a magnificent swimming pool which would remain unused by us all, because of the long hours worked. Just then, Simon came up to me and said 'Master, again thanks for a great day's work. Well done, everybody. We're scheduled to finish on time tomorrow. Now is 6 a.m. OK for breakfast?'

Of course it was. Three a.m. would be fine when you're having fun and respect your boss, safe in the knowledge that he values your hard work.

I've always remembered that lesson and thank my colleagues often for what they've done. I've sometimes forgotten in the rush of the day to thank my secretary, after racing through a pile of work together. So I phone Angela at home just to say 'thanks'. I know she appreciates it.

Try it. You'll feel better, and so will the person deserving of your praise. And remember, when you're paid a compliment, accept it! Put it in the bank. And the next time your confidence is put to the test, there will be enough of a reserve in the bank to stay in credit, with your confidence intact.

Summary

1   *Saying 'thank you and well done' demonstrates your appreciation. It raises your self-confidence and that of the person you're thanking.*

2   *It builds loyalty, while lack of recognition builds indifference.*

3   *When someone thanks you, accept his or her gratitude with good grace. Put it in the bank and watch your confidence grow.*

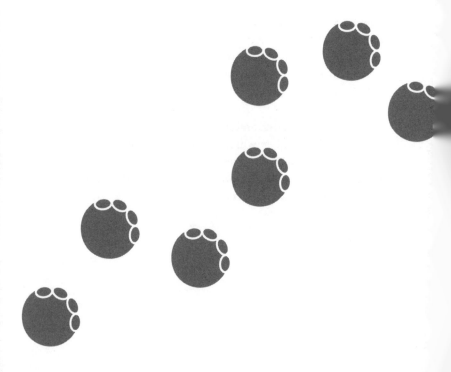

Chapter 7

Who Looks Stupid When You Criticize in Public?

*'Come mothers and fathers throughout the land … and don't
criticize what you can't understand.'*
Bob Dylan, 'The Times They are A-Changin''

If 'thank you and well done' is the right way to deal with praise,
how should we deal with criticism?

First, a confession. This is one I've often got wrong. Spectacu-
larly on one occasion when having dinner with my family one
summer's evening in the Scottish Highland town of Pitlochry.

I was there on business with a colleague and, while we worked
at the Diageo Blair Atholl distillery, Caroline took the children
round the local tourist attractions. We were all hungry by mid-
evening and frustrated by the lack of availability of tables in
restaurants.

It proved impossible to find a table for six and so, reluctantly, we
split into two groups of three in one eating place, with the kids
taking up position in one corner of the restaurant while Caroline, Jonathan and I occupied another.

As closing time approached, the children, one by one, sidled over to our table, bored and tired. The owner, meanwhile, began to use their table to pile up empty glasses from his now half-filled restaurant. At that point, the kids returned to their table to finish their drinks. As Emma, then 12, lifted her drink for a final sip, the owner bellowed across the restaurant '**Don't** play with the glasses. **(Pink Elephant!)** You'll break them.'

Now I know I should have gone over to him and explained patiently that my daughter was drinking from her own glass, pointing out politely that their table had been requisitioned as a clearing house for the restaurant's dirty dishes.

But for the same reasons that let me down with my half-chewed ticket in the car park – namely that I was tired and fresh out of professional politeness – I reacted differently.

Caroline and I rose together like a lion and lioness sensing that their cub was in danger.

'Excuse me,' I began loudly. (Basil Fawlty was consuming my character once more.)

'Perhaps if you had the courtesy to keep other people's dirty dishes off my children's table, you'd be able to see that they are drinking from their own glasses.'

Of course, that only provoked a worse reaction. '**Don't** tell me how to run my restaurant,' the now red-faced owner blasted back. **(Pink Elephant!)**

'You could obviously do with some advice,' I retorted, 'because you clearly have **no** clue about customer service. **(Pink Elephant!)** In fact, having witnessed your behaviour, I'd be surprised if any of these people here tonight would want to return.'

Around 30 people – probably enjoying a quiet night out – were now caught in a war zone. Each looked frightened to move, for fear of triggering off further sniping. Perhaps we ruined their meal. Perhaps we gave them a damn good laugh. Unquestionably, we provided them with a controversial talking point.

And how would they have viewed it? Well, probably most would have missed the initial salvo from the owner, so they would have been left joining the crossfire at my bizarre outburst. So I ask the question: who looks stupid when you criticize in public?

On reflection, I must have looked a plonker. In my rush to right a wrong, I broke the cardinal rule: criticize in private, praise in public. I'm sure a few of the diners were embarrassed by the experience. I'm certain my kids were mortified (yet again)!

Ironically, I left a good tip for the waitress who had been a delight to deal with. So I compounded the felony by praising her in private while criticizing her boss in public. At the very least, I could have done with remembering that when you point a finger at others, three of your fingers on the same hand are pointing back at you!

But when emotion rises, logic goes out the window – hence the Pitlochry 'scene'.

Even correcting your colleague, partner or friend in public over what you see as an incorrect fact is a mistake. Does it really matter that your wife said you were on holiday in July last year when in fact it was August? Why are you correcting her? Is it crucial to the story? And how does she now feel?

If your partner recalls a funny story from when the kids were younger, does it matter that your son was seven, rather than six at the time? How does your interjection help the telling of the story?

When your colleague says you were in Leeds last week for a meeting on a new project, do you really have to correct him and point out that it was a fortnight ago?

I've found myself attempting to justify my corrections, yet it only really matters if the slight inaccuracy leads to confusion or misinterpretation. Otherwise, let it go!

Wrong information offends our sense of right and wrong. But which is the greater crime: to get a fact wrong or to leave your partner, friend or business colleague angry, upset or embarrassed?

I now have one rule: if you would keep your mouth shut when a client makes a simple mistake, why would you dream of upsetting the people you love or respect most? The trouble is, it feels as if they'll accept your criticism most readily. But that's a pathetic excuse.

So the next time you're itching to correct in public, keep your mouth shut. You'll feel better for having exercised the self-restraint. As for praising in public, go back to 'thank you and well done' as the best non-medicinal tonic after a hard day's work.

We see it all too seldom. It strikes me that we need to have confidence to spare to be able to pass some on to our children, friends or colleagues. And, as most people in this country appear to lack confidence to some degree, praise comes with great difficulty.

I was golfing with a friend once who is more likely to greet a tremendous long-range shot to six feet from the flag with a comment such as 'just short', rather than 'great shot'. In the clubhouse afterwards, we were talking about our childhoods and he explained that his parents were cold people, who found it difficult to praise him, despite his obvious success in life.

That explained everything. He simply found it almost impossible to praise partners and opponents alike on the golf course, because he had little idea how to go about it. He was more used to hearing criticism and that's how his attempts at praise turned out.

I get frustrated watching wound-up fathers bellow criticism at their sons as we watch our kids play rugby or football on a Saturday morning. My son and his team-mates are often cold, wet, tired, frustrated – and sometimes losing. So do they really need to have their dwindling confidence further battered by middle-aged men who have failed to fulfil their own sporting ambitions?

Criticism is like a dagger to the heart of a youngster and to many an adult as well.

When I was eight years old, the man who was to be my only teacher for the next three years told me on my first day in his class 'McFarlan. You'll be a failure, just like your brother.'

Clearly my brother's three years in his class made little impact. Now a successful operator in the financial services industry, he barely remembers his teacher's jibes. But I have made it my goal since then to avoid criticism by producing work that exceeded expectations. And, if criticism is still forthcoming, I've found it hard to bear.

Criticism offends our sense of fairness. It often demonstrates a lack of respect for the intended target. And it's always worth considering the impact it will have before speaking out.

Caroline and I have made it our mission to praise the successes of our children and encourage them when things go wrong. Of course, like all parents, we also get it wrong. But it's worth remembering the wise words of an old adage: 'If a child lives with criticism, he learns to condemn.' It goes on to add 'If a child lives with encouragement, he learns confidence. If a child lives with praise, he learns to appreciate.'

Constructive criticism, delivered in private, is an entirely different matter. I've found that listening to constructive criticism of my work or behaviour has helped me improve on performance and attitude. So when delivering constructive criticism, make it the filling in a feedback sandwich, contained within positive reinforcement of what's going right.

People need to know what they're doing wrong, but they must also know how to correct their mistakes. Only offer criticism if you can suggest a better way of doing things.

So which kind of child, or employee for that matter, would you wish to be responsible for moulding? It's up to you. But in any situation, whether at home, at work or on a night out, who looks stupid when you criticize in public?

Avoid sarcasm (or had you managed to work that out for yourself?)

One hot day on holiday, our elder daughter Victoria swithered over whether to join us on a pedal boat in the bay or wait for us on the beach. The boat attendant, bored waiting for a decision, came out with a classic.

'Come on, come on. We're **not** all on holiday,' he suggested helpfully. (**Pink Elephant!**)

'Just as well some of us are,' I fired back. 'Otherwise you'd have all these boats to yourself.' (Yes, quite. Unhelpful sarcasm met with … more unhelpful sarcasm.)

Waiting to pick up Emma from a dancing class one dark night, I noticed a car sitting at right angles with its reverse lights on. A quick glance around assured me the driver had more than enough room to reverse past me. My thoughts returned quickly to the football match on the radio.

Another couple of minutes passed before an elderly gentleman left his driver's seat, opened his door and shouted across to me 'Exactly how long do I have to wait for you to move?'

Surprised at his tone, I made the situation worse by replying 'You could get a bus through there.'

'Well as I **don't** have a bus,' he continued **(Pink Elephant!)**, 'why **don't** you just move your car?' **(Pink Elephant!)**

To which I responded 'Tell me, at precisely what age does one become an old git?'

There I went again! It was the half-chewed, AIDS-ridden ticket scene all over again. Too much sarcasm, too little humility, total lack of apology. Personally, I blame it all on my primary school teacher.

The trouble is that sarcasm is like a sharp sword. One swift blow and your opponent can be cut in half. But why rush to use it? Isn't it enough to know you have a sharp sword handy for serious trouble without having to decapitate – metaphorically at least – an elderly man?

You must be so brave, Bill! Add his scalp to that of the ticket booth woman and the Pitlochry restaurant owner. Gosh I'm so proud to have shown them all! Oops, there I go again with the sarcasm!

My dear old gran used to tell me 'You're so sharp you'll cut yourself.' She was right, and I cut others who suffer the misfortune of stepping on my toes. But hold on. Did you learn as a child, as I did 'Sticks and stones will break my bones but names will **never** hurt me'? **(Pink Elephant!)**

Well, I feel the words of a poem by Barrie Wade on bullying to be far more appropriate. It begins:

> *'Sticks and stones may break my bones*
> *But words can also hurt me*
> *Stones and sticks break only skin*
> *While words are ghosts that haunt me.'*

Words can be tremendously hurtful, especially when hurled at you sarcastically. My resolution is to remember that sarcasm is the lowest form of wit … and leave it to Basil Fawlty, who's funnier with it anyway.

How do you define what's funny in any case? Do you laugh at every joke or 'funny' remark you ever hear?

In my experience, a remark has to be funny to both the teller AND the listener for it to be funny. And that's why self-deprecating humour is, in my view, the only safe humour. Jewish comedians can poke fun at Jewish habits. Black comics can laugh at their own race. Men can safely joke about men. But when humour is pointed outwards, rather than inwards, it can appear for all the world like a dangerous weapon.

When the jewellery chain boss Gerald Ratner cracked a joke or two about the quality of his products, he perhaps made the mistake of believing his humour was pointed inwards. After all, in describing the company's glassware as 'total crap', who else could be the butt of the joke but the Ratner Company? The remark was made to the Institute of Directors in 1991 during a speech in which Ratner also boasted that some earrings he sold were cheaper than a prawn sandwich, adding that the sandwich might last longer.

With considerable help from the *Sun* newspaper, who splashed the 'Total Crap' headline on page one, the humour backfired. Customers started to bring back their recent purchases, demanding their money back. Some complained that they felt the joke to be on them. Within weeks, the gaffe had badly affected business. In total, the joke was estimated to have wiped £500 million pounds off the value of the company, which Ratner left the following year and which removed his name from its outlets a further two years later.

One former Chief Constable of Strathclyde Police told a joke in the early days of his term of office at a cricket club dinner. However, when the joke was reported in the press, he was branded a 'racist'. I'm told by a fellow speaker at the dinner that the humour was appreciated both by the audience and by another principal guest, the great England all-rounder Basil D'Oliveira, who had suffered genuine racial abuse during his outstanding career.

Yet it looked bad when transferred to print, outside the atmosphere of that gathering. Several years later when the Chief Constable retired, the 'racist' tag was still being applied, like a bandage to a wound that refuses to heal. People who take offence often take a long time to forget. Sometimes they refuse to forgive.

Now, having placed this health warning on humour, I strongly believe that humour is sadly lacking in much of our communication. When I ask my friends and colleagues socially what's been happening in their day, they often choose to tell me the funniest incident, rather than the most important business news of the day.

But in a business setting, people often decide to play safe and avoid humour. In fact, they're playing dangerous and flirting with the real risk of their audience being bored by yet another humourless presentation. Some of the biggest earners in theatre and TV presentation are those with the greatest sense of humour. They're able to raise a smile on the collective face of their audience, with just a few well-chosen words.

One performance by a then recently-resigned Government minister demonstrated to me the power of self-deprecating humour. David Mellor's political progress was halted by damaging revelations about his personal life. His party – the Conservative government of the day – was highly unpopular in Scotland. The salacious detail dished in the tabloid newspapers' reporting of his political demise made for gross humiliation. Yet he stood before 500 sceptics in Glasgow, ripping his own reputation to shreds. He had the audience eating from his hand and received a standing ovation.

For humour to be effective, you have to consider how it will go down with the audience.

I was at a large, formal dinner when the guest speaker embarked on his 20-minute keynote speech. Much of it was dry and factual, but he decided to 'entertain' us with a joke. It turned out to be the most offensive anti-women joke I've ever had the misfortune to hear. Embarrassed for the two women at our table, I felt compelled, when he sat down, to remark 'And I thought Les Dawson was dead.' One entire table – comprising only women – walked out.

So how did he so misjudge the situation? Perhaps his humour was stuck in a bygone era. Perhaps he just failed to ask himself how the audience would react. Either way, he failed.

Another danger is having written the script, to follow it rigidly, regardless of audience reaction.

In delivering after-dinner speeches, I've often dropped a couple of stories immediately before using them because 'better' ones were received poorly. But I heard of a wedding where the bride's father plodded on with bad joke after bad joke, with little reaction from the audience. Until, that is, he turned a page after another eerie silence in response to a joke, to begin 'No, but seriously …' At which point, the gathering collapsed in laughter. At him, rather than with him.

My favourite humour is round-the-dinner-table wisecracking. That's where we've had great fun as a family. That's when keyed-up participants on a training course have dissolved in laughter. That's where a night out has become a scream. That's also where I've occasionally got into trouble for going overboard.

So use that sense of humour that most of us have, albeit sometimes hidden from view. And take one second to ask yourself if you would find it funny if you were on the receiving end.

Summary

1   *Destructive criticism of children and adults alike destroys their self-confidence and often turns them into critics themselves.*

2   *Only offer criticism privately – and ensure you're able to explain how things can be done better.*

3   *Humour's great. Just make sure everybody finds your humour funny.*

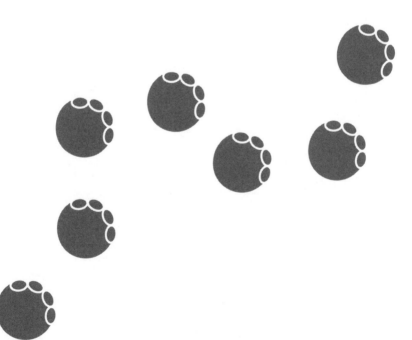

Section Three

Positively Assert Yourself

Chapter 8

Flush Out the Watering Down Words

'It is no use saying "we are doing our best." You have got to succeed in doing what is necessary.'
Winston Churchill

In Britain, we live with the curse of false modesty. Modesty, I believe, is a good thing. It often keeps events in perspective. A modest person will let you compliment her on her taste in clothes or the quality of her work, while a boastful equivalent will seek approval, often when it's less justified.

But by 'false modesty', what I mean is the need to preface any deed with a self-deprecating put-down like 'my dress sense is lousy', 'my spelling is terrible' or 'I'm a hopeless golfer.'

Some people do this all the time – to get their self-criticism in before, as they see it, others do. The reality is that they are usually the only ones who are critical.

However, most people indulge in a more subtle form of false modesty by watering down their remarks with endless – and useless – qualifications. The words they use are all members of the 'watering down' family – because they all dilute the message, every time.

They are words such as 'hopefully', 'probably', 'possibly', 'quite', 'relatively', 'reasonably' and 'fairly'. At times they can be joined by 'sometimes', 'seldom' and 'occasionally'.

Imagine that in a job interview you described yourself as 'reasonably' well-qualified for the job. 'Hopefully' you would fit in with the rest of the team, as you're 'fairly' good at working with others. You are 'probably' the right person for the job, and you can say that you're 'quite' punctual.

Personally, I would be shuffling through my papers by now, looking at the qualifications of the next candidate!

One evening, a few years ago, I agreed to back up a golfing friend of mine who was concerned after finding money missing from the gaming machine of his golf club. The golf club committee, to our surprise, was reluctant to take action against the person responsible for loading and unloading the machine. We met with the club captain to ask if he believed the employee in question was honest.

He thought about it for a while then turned to my friend and said 'Relatively honest.'

'*Relatively* honest,' I spluttered. 'And would I be *relatively* honest if I had played fair in the club championship final against you, but then cheated on the deciding hole?'

He reckoned that was a ridiculous question and pointed out that honest bar staff were hard to come by. I dug in and said that 'relatively' was an indictment of the individual's honesty. In fact, it emphasized their dishonesty.

My brother was delighted at the coverage a local newspaper had given to his training courses for would-be radio presenters. As he showed me the full-page spread, John asked me which word he now regretted having used.

I scanned the page. It was all very positive, apart from one little slip. '*Hopefully*, students will learn much from the course,' I suggested.

'Correct,' said John. 'I'm convinced they'll learn much, so why did I say "hopefully"?'

It was another case of false modesty and a good example of watering down the message.

Another way we do this is to begin each sentence with 'I think' when totally unnecessary. 'I think I can get an estimate for the repair work to you tomorrow,' is another cop-out. If you remove the 'I think', you've made a commitment. On occasions we use 'I think' instead of 'I firmly believe'.

However, 'I firmly believe this company will double in size within two years' is a courageous statement compared to 'I think this company will double in size within two years.' My money is on the bloke with the belief predicting his own positive future. Mind you, the bloke who only thinks it is also probably right!

Either way, it's perfectly acceptable to have a firm belief that proves to be wrong. It was after all a belief, rather than a fact. But what's wrong with daring to be right instead?

I'm sure we do this in Britain, and especially where I come from in the West of Scotland, to avoid being regarded as arrogant. It appears as if this fear is the driver behind the tone of our language. And yet, I have only met a handful of people I regard as truly arrogant, but thousands who lack self-confidence. Even then, I would put money on those who appear to be arrogant as also lacking self-belief.

Arrogance is easily spotted by the words people chose to describe themselves. Instead of saying 'I'm an experienced salesman', the arrogant person might say 'I'm a vastly experienced salesman.'

But false modesty would make that 'I'm a reasonably experienced salesman' when, after a lifetime in the business, the description is watered down to the point of being inaccurate.

So flush out the watering down words and take credit for what you've worked hard to achieve.

And while you're at it, do me the favour of removing two more pet-hate phrases. They are 'I'll try...' and 'I'll do my best.'

First of all, take this book and try to place it on the floor. Now, if you've laid it down, you've failed. I asked you to *try*. So by doing it, you've failed to *try*, if you see what I mean.

Why on earth then do we say to our children 'I'll try to pick you up at 8 o'clock'? That will only leave them unsure of when we'll be bothered to turn up.

I've done that myself, only to question why I left my daughter uncertain when all I had to do was tear myself away from the live football match on the television to be there on time. Would I do that to a client? Certainly not! So why do it to one of the people I love most in the world?

I once had dinner at a celebrity charity function I was hosting with the late Arne Naess, the Norwegian shipping magnate and mountaineer, who was married to international singing legend Diana Ross. Arne was telling me that he had to field calls constantly from the media about his transatlantic marriage, as Diana lived in the States while he spent most of his time in Britain. I later offered up some ways in which he might deal with the enquiries and suggested how he might reply to questions over the stability of the relationship.

Arne had me alternately in stitches and in stunned silence recounting tales from his fascinating life, but the biggest jaw-dropper came when he described the wedding ceremony with Diana. He told me 'When asked if I "would love and hold this woman, till death do you part", I replied "Well, I'll certainly *try* …"' His previous marriage had failed, he explained. He found it unrealistic to make a promise in the knowledge that it may turn out to be untrue. I read with sadness in February 2000 that Arne's explanation of his choice of words had become a self-fulfilling prophecy. The couple had divorced after a 14-year marriage.

Now when I started berating 'I'll do my best', during a training course, a good friend of mine jumped in and said he used the phrase all the time and believed in it. Steven ran a highly successful photographic business. His best would have been enough to keep his clients happy because of his excellent attitude to customer service.

However, I pointed out that *his* best and *my* best might be two entirely different things. To make the point, we acted out a long conversation in which I asked him for more film stock and he asked me first for payment owed to him. As the conversation drew to a close, Steven asked 'So can you pop in on Saturday with that cheque and I'll give you more film stock?'

I hesitated for a second and replied 'Steven, I'll do my best.'

Steven burst out laughing, conceding that *my* best would yet again fail to guarantee delivery of the cheque.

'I'll do my best' is often well-intentioned. But remember, the road to hell is paved with good intentions!

I phoned a courier company once, asking them to guarantee delivery of a parcel to a client for noon the following day. 'I'll do my best,' came the reply. Perhaps only 'I'll try' would have provoked a less favourable reaction.

'I'm sorry,' I replied, 'I'll need a commitment.'
'I'm telling you I'll do my best,' came the slightly offended re-sponse. 'I **can't** do any more than that. **(Pink Elephant!)**
'**Nothing's** guaranteed in this life, you know.' **(Pink Elephant!)**
'Well, unless you *can* guarantee delivery,' I replied, 'I will have to go elsewhere or deliver it myself. The choice is yours.'

It's all about taking responsibility. If he was unwilling to, I had to. I had made a commitment to my client. Clients sense that commitment when you remove the 'I'll do my best' phrase.

Potential employers want people who describe themselves as well-qualified for the job, who would fit in with the rest of the team as they're good at working with others, who are the right person for the job and who are punctual.

(Now, did you even notice the 'reasonably', 'hopefully', 'fairly', 'probably' and 'quite' missing that time? It just sounded altogether more committed.)

And, perhaps most importantly, your family will feel more secure in the knowledge that you'll be there for them when you remove the 'try to'.

Do your best to try to improve your commitment. You'll be reasonably impressed with the results … hopefully! At least, I think you will … sometimes.

Yes, no and I don't know

Caroline and I walked into a coffee shop in Charleston, South Carolina, looking for a good, strong cup of coffee after a long walk in the 90-degree heat outside. The attractive sales assistant looked delighted to see us and, it seemed, could hardly wait to tell us what she'd been doing.

'Hi there. How are you both this morning?' she enquired.
'I've just been dipping strawberries in chocolate. Would you like to try some?'

Well, with this personal invitation to indulge in her favourite pastime, backed up by her boundless enthusiasm, it would have appeared rude to have refused.

Sitting down with our coffees – and strawberries dipped in chocolate – we found ourselves $8 poorer than we had bargained for.

A travel-weary businessman, briefcase in hand and sweating profusely, was next to enter the shop. 'Good morning,' our friend began. 'I've just been dipping strawberries in chocolate. Would you like to try some?'
'No, I'll just have a tall latte to go please,' he replied firmly, but politely.

Did she burst into tears? Was she crushed by his rejection?

No, she simply smiled, said 'sure thing' and fixed his coffee.

Caroline and I just grinned to each other with a look that said 'What a couple of pushovers! We only wanted coffee, too.'

Saying 'no' got the sweaty businessman precisely what he wanted. Failure to say 'no' landed us with two over-hyped, overpriced, under-ripe chocolate-covered strawberries.

Back in Britain, I see endless shoppers scuttling away from volunteers collecting for charities, pretending they are deaf, rather than saying 'no thanks' to an appeal for contributions. But then, people tell me they feel very negative when they reply 'no' to several consecutive questions. Even when the correct answer is indeed 'no'.

Of course, if you stop there, it is negative. It's simply a dead-end answer. So what you have to do is find the positive solution, rather than stop on the negative problem.

We had a handyman come to estimate the cost of painting the eaves of our house. It's a tricky job. So, when the painter arrived, I had a bet on with Caroline that he would find a reason to avoid doing it.

The chap took one look at the high side of the house and said: 'Oh dear. I **don't** have a ladder big enough.' **(Pink Elephant!)** Attempting to help him to the solution, I asked if he knew where he could get one. 'No' was his clear and negative answer. And that was the end of the debate.

The next painter who came to price the job also hesitated when he saw the height of the eaves. 'Do you have a long enough ladder?' I asked, more in hope than in expectation this time.

'No,' he replied. 'But I've got a mate who has one, and I'm sure I can borrow it for a few days.'

Problem solved. He also began his answer with 'no', but continued until he found the solution.

Peter, by the way did an excellent job in painting the eaves, using his borrowed ladder. It was also he who dropped the white paint from the highest point of the house on to the steps and retrieved the situation with his Regret, Reason and Remedy.

So 'no' is a perfectly acceptable start to an answer. Similarly, so is 'yes', but its omission can cause problems.

If one of your colleagues asked if you liked a report he had written, how do you think this answer would go down?

'It was interesting. Different from the way I would have written it, but interesting.'

I reckon he would be upset by your unwillingness to commit to a clear response. But if you said:

'Yes I did. It was interesting. Different from the way I would have written it, but interesting,' then I believe he would feel you had given him a direct answer.

'Yes' is a powerful word.

My daughter, in finishing a part-time job while studying at university, was asked by a colleague if Victoria regarded her as a bully.

'Yes, I believe you are a bully,' was Victoria's blunt and brave response. The other girl was shocked and went on the defensive. We agreed the girl had only asked her the question to have Victoria deny her colleague's behaviour publicly. The tactic backfired and the girl felt the full power of the word 'yes'.

That leaves as an alternative to 'yes' and 'no', a third choice: 'I don't know.'

And here's a thing. Despite a good school education, a qualification in journalism and more than a quarter of a century working in newspapers, radio and television, despite an insatiable thirst for news and current affairs and a deep interest in the business of my clients, as well as the lives of my friends and colleagues, I have a confession to make.

What I know is a drop in my ocean of ignorance.

And what should I do about this ignorance? Cover it up? Pretend I really do know when I don't?

Or just admit it and seek to find out the answer to the question I'm being asked?

I go for the last option every time. So why are so many of us terrified to use these three honest little words: 'I don't know'?

It seems the higher some people climb in commerce and industry, the more pressure they feel to avoid that phrase. Again, if it's repeated often, like 'no', then it can feel negative.

One interviewee admitted to me after a training session 'I just hated saying "I don't know" to so many of your questions.'

I reminded him of the consequences of bluffing his way out of that position, by pretending to know something he was so obviously unclear on. If we start to bluff, we make things up. If we make things up, we lie. If we lie, we're branded a liar. And, once branded a liar, it takes a long time to shake off the tag.

I also pointed out that 'I don't know' was indeed the correct answer to my questions and that he had gone on each time to explain what he did know. So a section of the interview went like this:

'How many jobs will be lost?'

'I don't know. The scale of the cutbacks will be determined by our sales in the next quarter. Only when that's known can we put a final figure on it.'

'And will these be the last cutbacks?'

'I don't know. The market has fluctuated greatly in recent years. When there's been high demand for our product, we've been pleased to take on new recruits. When demand has dropped, sadly we've had to let people go.'

Stopping at the 'I don't know' would have sounded negative, defensive and even abrasive. But following up each phrase with a fuller explanation is helpful and lends more understanding to the subject matter. In isolation, 'I don't know' is the problem. But when followed up with what you do know, it's the launch pad to the solution. Using it means you've told the truth and given what limited information you have available.

If you think you can avoid answering 'yes', 'no' or 'I don't know' to some questions, ask the former Home Secretary Michael Howard how he felt after being interviewed on BBC's *Newsnight* by Jeremy Paxman in 1996.

Paxman asked the Home Secretary direct questions 14 times about the resignation of the Director of Prisons, Derek Lewis. Fourteen times, Michael Howard refused to give a direct answer to a direct question. He looked as slippery as an eel and every duck and dive, every avoidance of 'yes', 'no' or 'I don't know' made a bad situation worse.

In truth, the next news item on *Newsnight* was unavailable and its loss had left the producer with a hole to be filled. So the Home Secretary's waffling was helping out the producer enormously. Some political commentators, however, reflecting on Howard's failure to become the next Tory leader at that time, highlighted that night on *Newsnight* and his handling of the Derek Lewis affair as a crucial turning point in his fortunes.

Summary

1   Remove the words that dilute your message – words like 'quite', 'relatively', 'hopefully', 'fairly' and 'reasonably'.

2   'I'll do my best' and 'I'll try' both lack firm commitment.

3   To avoid sounding evasive, where possible begin an answer with 'yes', 'no' or 'I don't know'.

Chapter 9

Talk Positively About Yourself

'Remember, no-one can make you feel inferior without your consent.'
Eleanor Roosevelt

How do you reply when somebody asks you the question 'How are you?' I'm fascinated by the variety of answers I hear. Each one gives an insight into the respondent.

One evening, I was one of a large number of parents at my children's school, on hand to give advice to pupils on the careers we all had followed. Twelve pupils wanted to know about a career in broadcast journalism. Each had been allocated a ten minute slot with me to ask questions.

As each came into the room, I asked exactly the same question: 'How are you?' The variety of answers from these 15-year-olds was very interesting.

The first lad responded in a typically Scottish manner '**Not** bad, thanks.' **(Pink Elephant!)**

The next, a girl, was only marginally better with 'Oh, I'm fine.' Neutral, I would say.

It was the third who really worried me. 'Hello John. How are you?' I asked.
'Oh, surviving,' he answered. 'But for how much longer?' I pondered.

I ask you! What kind of a response is that? Sadly it's the kind of response our children hear from us all the time.

I can almost understand British understatement. But 'surviving'? As in from a natural disaster or nuclear fallout? It really made me question what his parents were teaching him. How would they respond to the same question? Was he just acting 'cool' in case his peers saw him?

My dad, now in his eighties, is positive by nature. But his response to that question used to let him down. He had spent all his life answering 'not bad'. A few years ago, I took him to task on it.

'How are you?' I enquired as usual.
'Oh, not bad,' came the predictable reply.
'Would you say you're healthy?' I asked further.
'Yes I'm fine,' he agreed.
'And would you say your savings are sufficient to make you comfortable?' I probed.
'Yes. But what's with the inquisition?' he demanded.
'One final question,' I persisted. 'Would you describe yourself as "happy"?'

'Yes, I'm happy,' he replied. 'But what point are you trying to make?'

'Well, what I want to know is this: is "not bad" really the best way to describe your circumstances?' I concluded.

'And what do you suggest I say?' he asked, somewhat niggled by my final question.

'I would reckon that "I'm very well thanks, and how are you?" would be far more apt.'

A fortnight went by before we next met up and my dad had some interesting news for me.

'By the way,' he started. 'People think I've had a triple heart bypass.'

Confused, I wondered what on earth he was talking about. 'A triple heart bypass?' I replied curiously. 'And why do they think that?'

'Because,' he said triumphantly, 'when people ask how I am, I now say "I'm very well thanks, and how are you?"' According to my dad, this was normally met with a very positive remark about his chirpiness these days, and the suggestion that his new lease of life might be related to a major heart operation!

Your response to the question 'how are you' is really a launch pad. If the answer is 'not bad', the rocket's likely to remain grounded. If it's 'oh, surviving', I would suggest that the engine's on fire.

My dad discovered that his positive responses launched the conversation into encouraging comments about his health and attitude to life that are only a fair reflection of how he feels about life in his eighties.

As a footnote to the school careers night, the last lad to pop in to see me had replied to my question by saying 'I'm very well, thanks. How are you?'

That led to me passing on this tip about answering that question.

Ironically, he was the one young adult that night who already had his answer sorted. It was the others who needed to work on theirs.

Habits adopted at such tender years stick with us for life. I'm constantly amazed at how negatively front-line staff in restaurants, shops, office receptions and hotels greet their clients.

Walking into one five-star hotel on business recently, I asked the duty manager how he was. 'Hanging by a thread!' came his triumphant response. Please, somebody, hand me the scissors and put the poor man out his misery! Worse still, one seminar delegate told me his former colleague used to end every day with the same pronouncement: 'Oh well. Another day closer to death!'

How we describe ourselves has a huge influence on our audience. I've heard several women, when asked what they do for a living, describe themselves as '*just* a housewife and mother'. By contrast, one friend, also a stay-at-home mum, described herself as 'Head of Personal Development'. Most parents would agree with that description.

Unnecessary self-criticism is most obvious to me when I ask people to analyse their own performance in a TV interview on one of our media training courses. Typically, the interviewee will begin 'I thought I was a bit woolly in the answers … struggled to find the

right words ... too many "ums" and "ehs" ... poor grammar ...'
When I ask others to analyse the same interview, they may say
'On the contrary, I felt it was fluent, to the point, interesting ...'

However, when we visit France, Spain and the United States to
run similar exercises, the participants most often list what they did
well first, then turn to their perceived faults. Their self-assessments
tend to be more realistic than those of their British counterparts.

It's very difficult to have a healthy perspective of your own performance. It's also difficult to remain positive about yourself when
you've had a day wading through the treacle of life. But if you
become negative about yourself, it will quickly rub off on those
around you. They may quickly mark you down as having low
self-esteem, which in turn may reduce your chances of getting
that job, arranging a meeting or simply being good company.

I'm all for self-deprecating humour at the start of a speech when
the audience has to be won over. But stay positive about yourself at all times and people will enjoy your company far more. So
when you ask someone how he or she is, do you really want to
be told 'oh, surviving' or would you rather hear 'I'm very well
thanks, and how are you?'

Be positive and proactive, especially with bad news

I was puffing and panting in the corner of the squash court, having been taken apart by an opponent in the first game of a best-
of-five set. It was a league match and I had about 15 minutes to
avoid myself crashing to an unexpected 3–0 defeat.

I say 'unexpected', because I had gone on court expecting to win. The league positions showed I had more points accumulated over the winter than my opponent and, while it was our first meeting, I had taken the court anticipating success.

Crucially, however, my opponent had gone on court expecting to lose. And even after crushing me in the opening game, he was clearly harbouring negative thoughts. I know that because he told me so.

Breathing normally in sharp contrast with my impersonation of a 60-a-day smoker, he said 'I'm pleased to have won that first game. I expected to lose 3–0, so I **can't** do worse than lose by 3–1 now.' **(Pink Elephant!)** His words were music to my ears. I decided, despite the early setback, that we should share his expectation of a 3–1 defeat.

As I walked off court, breathing more easily after turning the game round to win 3–1, I was asked by my opponent if I could point out any weakness in his game. 'Your game is very similar to mine,' I suggested, 'but I would beware of sharing a prediction of defeat with your opponent. Because once you'd said that, we had a pact.'

We set ourselves expectations all the time. If, while driving along a bumpy road, you spot a pothole, avoiding it can prove difficult.

'**Don't** hit the pothole' (**Pink Elephant!**) is an instruction to the brain involving 'hit' and 'pothole'. It's easy to see why we so often wreck the suspension on our cars with such an instruction. It's even worse if you spot a half-brick on the road while riding a motorbike or cycling along. Your mind seems to focus on the obstacle and hit it.

Golfing in Portugal with two friends, Gary was first on the tee and surveyed the 200 yards of water between where he stood and the green. 'Right,' he proclaimed. 'Put this in the heart of the green!'

The ball soared up into the azure-blue sky and landed 20 feet from the flag.

Our higher-handicap playing partner was next up, clearly dreading what lay ahead.

'Now **don't** put this in the water!' he instructed himself, in classic Pink Elephant style.

The ball launched, curved ... and splashed in the middle of the lake.

He turned in disgust, placed a second ball on the tee and, before I could say anything, repeated his mantra.

'Now for God's sake, **don't** put this one in the water!'

SPLASH!

I then teed up, looked at the flag and announced: 'Right ... inside Gary's ball!'

My ball took off, flew over the water, hit the green and landed a couple of feet closer to the flag than Gary's.

Now, ability and practice count for much on the golf course, but so does visualization of the shot. We *all* got the result we visualized.

When Tiger Woods embarked on his professional golf career after achieving phenomenal success as an amateur, he was asked what his realistic expectations were from his first pro tournament.

He told the interviewer – former US Open Champion Curtis Strange – that he turned up at every tournament believing he would win. Strange chuckled and suggested that Woods would learn. But four days later, it was Strange who was eating humble pie, as Woods won his debut tournament as a professional. He went on to win the US Masters at the first attempt and later won the four 'major' tournaments of world golf consecutively.

Unusually, I heard Tiger being defensive on the eve of the bi-annual USA-Europe Ryder Cup, played at the Belfry near Birmingham in September 2002.

Ahead of his opening match, he told the interviewer 'It's **not** a matter of life and death.' **(Pink Elephant!)** Adding '**Nobody's** being taken hostage.' **(Pink Elephant!)**

Uncharacteristically, Tiger had been taken hostage – by the Pink Elephants!

More used to being single-minded and thoroughly positive, he played the first two matches with a partner and (judging from the interview) with low expectations. He lost both matches.

In any other tournament I've seen him play, all the evidence would suggest that Tiger Woods thinks as positively as he talks. He talks himself into success, rather than out of it. For him, the bottle is definitely half-full, rather than half-empty.

My son was helping me to clear up one morning after a late-summer barbecue. Andrew shouted across the patio 'What do you want me to do with the half-full wine bottles, Dad?'

'Just put them in the kitchen, please,' I replied.
'And what about the half-empty ones?' he teased.
'There are none,' I replied. 'They're all half-full.'

It's easier, of course, to be positive before an event and after a victory, whether in sport or in life. But what do you do when the news is bad?

Well, that takes us back to Regret, Reason and Remedy. Say you're sorry for the way things worked out. Explain what happened. Then suggest what you'll do next to improve the situation.

It may feel easier to hide in these circumstances, but it takes courage to deal with the Three Rs and it wins respect among those listening.

I have the utmost admiration for Gavin Hastings, who captained the Scottish rugby team during the 1990s with dignity and resolve. At one point, Scotland suffered a string of defeats, but Gavin refused to buckle. His Regret, Reason and Remedy left the critics unable to question his attitude and it got him through the sticky times on to others when success came more easily.

I vividly remember interviewing a Scottish football manager, Alex Smith, the day he was sacked by St. Mirren FC. How readily would you agree to a BBC TV interview if you had just been sacked? You may be feeling angry, sick, despondent or all three. And a reporter wants you to rake over the coals. Alex had my greatest respect that day and my sympathy as well. If I remember correctly, he also faced the media when losing his job at Aberdeen and Dundee United. His dignity remained intact.

What Alex Smith and Gavin Hastings had in common was that both were proactive in the face of defeat. Rather than reacting to criticism by refusing to speak, they both came out calmly to explain their position.

Many of my clients have chosen to be proactive in announcing job losses or product recalls. That way they can remain in control of what's being said, because they are the ones who are saying it.

One, the cable company Telewest (then United Artists) had to deal with the tragedy of three workmen being crushed under a wall that collapsed on top of them as they dug a trench. One was dead and two were seriously injured. The public relations officer (PRO) phoned for advice on what to say to the media, if anything. The contractors who employed the men were refusing to comment. United Artists felt, rightly in my view, that they had to fill the silence.

I asked the PRO 'Do you regret what's happened?'
'Absolutely,' she replied. 'We're all devastated about the accident.'
'What caused it?' I asked.

'It's really much too early to say for certain,' she told me. 'But we've already started our investigations and we're helping the police at the scene with theirs.'

'And what will you do to prevent a further injury or loss of life?' I enquired.

'We've stopped work on the site until we find out what's happened. Then we'll be in a position to take action to ensure this sort of accident is prevented in the future.'

Unwittingly, she had just constructed her statement to the media, based on the Three Rs.

Proactively, she went with the statement to the media and as I drove home from a speaking engagement at midnight that night, I heard her words repeated on the local radio station. She would have been entitled to decline to comment, as it was really down to the contractors to do so. But her decision to be proactive was the right one and led to fair and reasonable coverage in the media.

Caroline and I faced an upsetting and sensitive situation, six days before a huge charity concert we had been planning for more than a year.

We received a call to say that our Master of Ceremonies for *Blast from the Past* – a reunion of top bands from the 70s – had died suddenly.

MUD's Les Gray had been fighting cancer, but was due to make a stage comeback to help raise money for Caroline's umbrella charity, KidsCharities UK.

Shocked by what we'd learned and concerned about the possible perception of fans that the concert could be called off, we decided to go on the front foot and be proactive with the sad news.

We left it 24 hours so relatives could be informed, then sent out a news release announcing that the bands would be turning the concert into a tribute to Les Gray. His widow Carol appreciated the gesture, the media gave widespread coverage to the story – and the concert went down a storm with the 1200 people who came along.

Assuming versus checking

Several days after my return from a business trip, the travel agent phoned to ask if everything had gone smoothly. 'Yes it did,' I began, 'although we got off to a bad start because of the absence of tickets. I phoned your office,' I continued, 'when I discovered on the Sunday we were leaving that they had failed to arrive, but it was closed.'

The travel agent was clear and precise in her reply. 'My records show that we left a message on your answering machine three days before departure, at which point we assume you're then aware that the tickets are in our office ready for collection.'
'And what would happen,' I teased, 'if I failed to hear about the tickets?'
'Well we *assume* you did, because we left a message,' she retorted.
'The machine was faulty,' I replied. 'Your message failed to record.'
'Well we just *assume*…' She tailed off, unable to find where to go next with her reply. Now, I take responsibility for my faulty

answering machine. I take responsibility for forgetting to check up on the whereabouts of tickets. The travel agent, however, must take responsibility for her assumption.

And that sums up the difficulty with assuming. It jumps to a conclusion that may well be false because it considers communication to be complete when it's only just started.

On that basis, if I send a letter I should assume that it arrives and that its contents are understood and acted on. By the same logic, on presenting news and sports bulletins in the past, I should assume that everybody watched, everybody understood and everybody could repeat exactly what I had said, conveying the full meaning of the information. That's a whole lot of assuming!

We're all guilty of assumptions. The highly-experienced TV journalist John Stapleton, now a GMTV presenter, tells a great story to make the point. While working late shift in the newsroom one night, he took his turn to go to reception to collect the Chinese carry-out ordered by his colleagues.

John approached the chap sitting in reception and took out some cash, saying 'Hi. Where's the carry-out?' The fellow looked at him blankly, so he elaborated 'Chinese carry-out?'

The gentleman replied slowly 'I am the Prime Minister of Singapore.'

Here's an alternative to assuming: how about just checking that the message is received and understood and that your facts are correct?

Summary

1   Start describing your life positively and watch the interest grow.

2   Be positive in the face of bad news. By breaking the news, you remain in control of what's being said first.

3   Instead of assuming, check the facts.

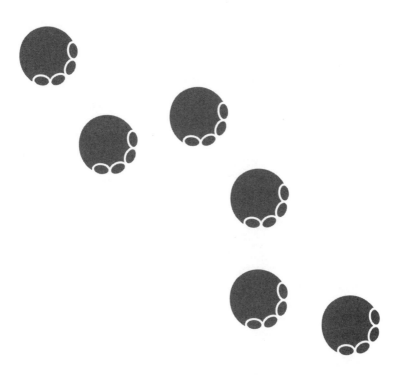

Think of the Audience

Chapter 10

It's All Relative

'Don't Sweat the Small Stuff ... and it's all Small Stuff.'
Richard Carlson, book title

You're standing at a party, drink in hand, music playing, two days before Christmas. Yet, despite the reason to be cheerful, you're bored out of your skull. The person who has cornered you is in full flow, talking about people whose names and lives are alien to you.

'David's my second cousin on my mother's side. When mother moved from Little Hockstead in 1977, she met David's dad for the first time in years. Harry was an electrical engineer who had a son and a daughter ... David and Claire, who's three years younger than David. In fact, Claire's got two of her own now. Jason is six and little Anna is just five months old ... or is it six now?'

Who cares how old Anna is! You find it impossible to work out this family tree, given that every single name is unfamiliar to you. In fact, your only use for the family tree right now is to hang yourself from it, or, better still, hang the bore who has driven you to this state of mind.

How can anybody be so boring? It's easy, really. If you fail to make your story relate to the person you're talking to, they will almost certainly be bored to tears, unable to form a picture in their mind of what the hell you're talking about.

It's back to the old issue of speaking in pictures.

You're sitting at home in Britain watching the weather forecast. How interesting is the weekend forecast for southern Spain? Extremely, if that's where you're headed on holiday tomorrow! And once in Spain, how interesting is the forecast for Britain? It's probably of limited appeal unless, of course, you wish to gloat over your good fortune.

Ready to return home, the British forecast is suddenly of interest once more. It's all a question of relevance. It has to relate to you.

Sadly, the loss of 100 lives in a train crash in India will hold little interest to a British audience. Yet when far fewer people died at Ladbroke Grove in London when an express train was in collision with a commuter train, the news dominated bulletins and newspapers for weeks. The consequences impacted on everybody who used a train in Britain, as major repair works caused delays. It related to them.

So music idols and sports stars sell newspapers because their fans are interested. Tiger Woods' picture sells golf magazines. David Beckham sells English tabloid newspapers. And, in the summer, when football's on holiday, the tennis circus rolls into town and tennis players sell newspapers – because the tennis is happening at Wimbledon in London, rather than Melbourne, Australia.

I was well aware of the need to grab an interview with Jack Nicklaus, Seve Ballesteros, Greg Norman or Nick Faldo for my BBC reports, when covering the Open golf championship each year. The chances were that one of them would be in contention on the Sunday afternoon. It's all about finding what your audience can relate to.

This explains why you'll find dozens of men sitting on benches outside ladies' clothes shops in malls each Saturday and Sunday, staring blankly into space. Unable to relate to the contents of the shops they're lost in their own thoughts, to which they can relate perfectly.

Most teenage boys will want to watch on television the sports they play, or go to the cinema to see films about teenage boys and girls. Many teenage girls want to talk to their friends about people like them, or watch a film about – you've guessed it – teenagers. Most women glaze over when their partners salivate over the curve on a glorious free kick into the top corner of the net. Most golfers glaze over when you insist on describing your great round, shot by shot. Especially if it's over a course with which they're unfamiliar. (It's like second cousin David's extended family.)

Five-time Open Golf Champion Tom Watson has a useful expression for this endless prattle. He calls it 'golf mouth'.

Because we need to relate to a news story, most of us find the foreign affairs of small African nations difficult to understand. As we're unlikely to go there on holiday – and barely understand where the countries are – these stories are often buried on page two or four of papers, beside the farming round up. Unless, of course, foot and mouth disease sweeps Britain, preventing us from walking in the countryside. Then farming's on the front page, because it involves us.

And if a terrorist, believed to be operating from Afghanistan, is blamed for the Twin Towers attack, suddenly the geography of Afghanistan, the movements of Osama bin Laden and his al Qaeda organization become our business. It becomes our grave concern when the threat is extended to our country.

If there is one question covering all of this it is simply 'What's in it for me?' The answer may be education, enlightenment or entertainment when hearing something new. But there must be something to grab your interest. Journalists call it a 'hook' or a 'peg' to hang the story on.

I, for one, failed to get to grips with the wars that tore the Balkans apart after the break up of Yugoslavia in the 1990s. The trouble is that the media struggled to explain the complexities in regions seldom – if ever – visited by Brits. The information was all there in the broadsheet newspapers and on our screens. When one atrocity followed another, when one mass grave was discovered, followed by another, we took note that it was terrible. But we could seldom remember where it had happened, let alone why.

The media knows it has to keep the audience interested or they go elsewhere. Hence, at least in part, the reason for the 'dumbing down' of much of our TV and newspaper coverage. (Curiously, radio at the same time has managed to widen its appeal because, while targeting its audience more clearly, it has continued to offer intelligent debate. It also helps that, in contrast to TV and newspapers, radio can be enjoyed while driving. In this time-conscious world, there's a premium on doing two things at the one time.)

At the time when the Balkans were awash with atrocities, the tabloids in Britain were giving mass coverage to the dog that barked at a postman, leading to a magistrate ordering that the dog be destroyed. We can envisage a dog barking at a postman, but we struggle to understand the ethnic issues behind the Balkan tensions.

When opening up a conversation or the address to a meeting or conference, just ask yourself what would be the most interesting point to begin with if you were in the audience. That's where to start the conversation or presentation. It can go wherever you want to go from there, but it's the starting point or 'hook'.

I once listened to a radio piece with growing mirth as the interviewer went round in circles, attempting to find a hook for his audience to allow them to relate to the story. Radio Five Live's highly accomplished John Inverdale was talking to a Finnish journalist about the unusually high number of elks killed on Finnish roads each year.

'Ten thousand elks killed each year by motorists,' began John. 'What's the reason?'

'Well elk meat is very popular,' came the reply, 'and so the Government believes motorists are deliberately knocking down elks so they can eat them.'

'Really,' replied John. 'And for those of us who are unfamiliar with elk meat … and I suppose that's most of us … what does it taste like?'

'Well it's strong and distinctive,' said the journalist.

'Right. So, what would you compare it to,' grappled Inverdale.

'I don't know,' said the journalist. 'As I say, it's difficult to compare.'

'Well, perhaps like venison,' offered the presenter.

'No, it's different to venison,' came the unhelpful reply.

Now desperate to make the interview work before disappearing down the plughole, Inverdale offered increasingly unlikely comparisons, each dismissed by the interviewee.

And then, the Finnish journalist finally offered a comparison.

'I suppose elk tastes rather like *bear*.'

There was a stunned silence, followed by a tone that brought resignation and mischief together.

'Well there you are ladies and gentlemen,' concluded the presenter. 'Elk tastes like *bear*.'

John Inverdale knew you have to catch the attention before it wanders. In other words, make it relate, before it's too late.

Put it into perspective

It was a glorious summer's day as my partner and I fought to keep up with our golfing opponents over the King James the Sixth course at Perth in Central Scotland. I hit a big drive on to the front edge of the green of a short par-four. But instead of winning the hole, I three-putted merely to halve the hole. (I know this is 'golf mouth' but bear with me.)

I was angry with myself for putting so badly, missing an opportunity to draw closer to our opponents and for letting my partner down.

Then I considered something that put this 'catastrophe' into perspective. A friend of ours was fighting a losing battle against cancer. What she would have given for a three-putt to be the biggest problem in her life. Immediately, I felt ashamed at my selfishness and resolved to put my mistake in perspective. On the next tee, I hit another good shot, then holed a long putt to win the hole.

Perspective is a wonderful thing. But it's very difficult to maintain when emotion takes over and logic disappears out the door.

My favourite book on the subject is Richard Carlson's excellent *Don't Sweat the Small Stuff* (even though it's a **Pink Elephant!**). In it, he makes the point about a plate being smashed in the kitchen. Some people get very upset about such incidents. But surely it's worth considering that either you will outlast the plate or it will outlast you. Which would you rather have happen?

I've adopted his philosophy time and time again when getting upset about nothing. I sometimes get frustrated when taking a wrong turning while driving abroad on holiday. And if I forget to keep things in perspective, Caroline will remind me that we are, after all, on holiday and time is more plentiful than when we're at home.

'On the scale of things,' I sometimes ask out loud, 'how important is it really?' Looking at scale is often the key to seeing how small the issue is.

And some of the most effective campaigns have used scale brilliantly. 'Seven pence a day is all it takes to feed a child in Ethiopia,' one such campaign told us. Now that really does put things into perspective!

On a visit to Las Vegas, we visited the nearby Hoover Dam. The human achievement in creating the dam was enormous and it is so large that we found it impossible to find a camera angle that showed the scale of the dam.

But two perspectives on display there I found unforgettable:

1   The lake created by the dam holds enough water to flood the whole of New York State to a depth of one foot.

2   There's enough concrete in the dam to build a four-foot-wide path round the world at the Equator.

These scales allow us to form a mental picture. They give us a comparison.

When working with the senior management of Cunard, as they prepared to launch the world's biggest passenger ship, the *QM2*, we rehearsed some comparisons.

- If you stood on the top deck of the *QM2* sailing into Manhattan, you'd be able to look the Statue of Liberty in the eye.

- If placed in the middle of Manhattan, the *QM2* would stretch for more than four blocks.

Do you see how the perspective expressed as a clear picture brings the scale to life?

The ship, by the way, weights 150,000 tonnes. But if you can explain to me what that's like, I'd be grateful. (I wonder how many elks that would be?)

I suggest to my clients that they put temporary downturns into perspective. When announcing 200 job losses, for example, it's crucial to say that the redundancies are necessary to safeguard the 1000 jobs remaining at the plant. It's also worth pointing out that numbers have risen and fallen throughout the company's 75 years in the area. One statement gives a sense of scale in numbers, while the other gives an indication of history in perspective.

Many people complain to me about media coverage of events. They know they're annoyed but find it difficult to know what's bugging them. The answer is often loss of perspective.

What's annoying to some people is the prominence some stories – like that of the condemned dog – receive. Others are fed up with the huge interest in football stories. Others wonder why a member of the royal family 'only has to sneeze', as they would put it, for it to be headline news. Some are puzzled by why soap stars constantly adorn the front pages of tabloids. Again, it's all a question of perspective. When a story receives too much prominence for some people's liking, perspective is lost.

But before we get too hot under the collar about the media, it's worth remembering how we behave ourselves. How we are angered by three-putting. How we lose our temper when a plate falls and smashes. How taking a wrong turning on a road can feel like a natural disaster.

It's all too easy to lose perspective in the heat of the moment.

My first visit to New York City was in 1996. I was there to run another media training course for the Cunard shipping company, but had the family with me as we were going on elsewhere. Having got to know the city better now, I find it one of the most vibrant places on earth, and feel perfectly safe there. But before that first visit, we had previously avoided the city when in the States as we perceived it to be dangerous.

So we were just a little on edge as we arrived in Manhattan. And we had been in that cauldron of noise beneath those imposing skyscrapers for literally five minutes when Andrew, then nine, said he wanted to cross the road to look at a shop. My wife and I were preoccupied attempting to sort out car hire details outside a rental shop and the request pushed Caroline's panic button.

'Andrew, just please stand there and **don't** move,' **(Pink Elephant!)** she snapped. 'People get shot dead in New York.'

For five minutes, we sorted through airline tickets, driving licences and hotel reservations before finally finding the car rental paperwork. Caroline turned to the children only to find Emma in tears. 'What's wrong now?' she asked.

'I **don't** want to get shot dead,' **(Pink Elephant!)** came the distressed response.

Loss of perspective led to the initial remark. And Caroline's general observation had become a living nightmare for a terrified 10-year-old.

We look back on incidents like these and ask ourselves: 'How could we possibly have made such a mistake?' Can we forgive ourselves for terrifying a child or snapping off the head of a car park attendant?

Now if Regret, Reason and Remedy should be sufficient when explaining your deeds to others, perhaps it should be accepted readily when you're the one who's been let down.

So put it into perspective, especially when it comes down to what you expect of yourself.

Summary

1   *For anything to be interesting, we need to relate to it.*

2   *What's interesting to us may well be boring to our audience.*

3   *Put a problem into perspective to see how small it really is.*

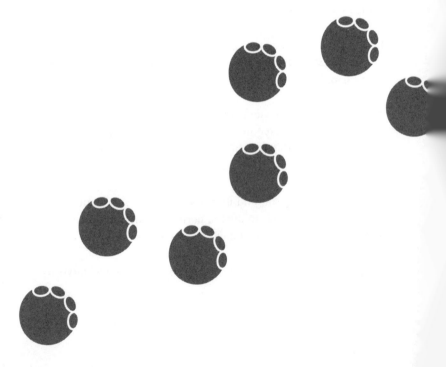

Chapter 11

Email and Text – Bullets or Boomerangs?

'Don't tell Anna.'
Text message sent by mistake to … Anna, 2001

I find emailing a tremendous way to communicate – for certain occasions. For firing off a quick confirmation of an arrangement or quoting for a piece of work and receiving an instant reply at bullet-fast speed, it is tremendous.

But beware the critical or apparently underhand message that comes back and hits you like a boomerang on the back of the neck.

Government press officer Jo Moore discovered this lesson to her cost when, within an hour of the second plane hitting the Twin Towers in New York on 11 September 2001, she sent out an email suggesting this was a good time to 'bury' bad Government news.

She later had to apologize for her actions which, with the perspective that time brings, made her look callous and calculating. The media had a field day, suggesting that she was a liability to her boss, the already embattled Transport Secretary, Stephen Byers.

Five months later, with press comment still rumbling on from the September email, a further row broke out about Transport Department emails. Newspaper reports suggested that Moore was rebuked in a new email for planning to release damaging rail figures on the day of the funeral of the Queen's younger sister, Princess Margaret.

Amid Government denials of its very existence, Moore's colleague Martin Sixsmith refused to buckle and maintained the email had been written. Soon after, Stephen Byers and Jo Moore stepped down ... their careers derailed by emails. Internal memos had become newspaper, radio and TV headlines.

I've seen email communication that grown men and women should be ashamed of. One I saw from an Internet company director, in answer to a certain criticism, began 'Up Yours'! I reckon the sender was a little upset when he wrote it. I wonder how he felt on reading it a month later.

I once sent a long explanation of why I was disappointed at the way a colleague in an associated company had treated a member of my staff. While pointing out my disappointment, I asked that we all pull together on the project to ensure its success. The reply to my 300-word message was itself only four words long: 'Duly noted – and binned.'

My secretary was wise enough to shield me from its contents to stop me firing an even bigger cannon back. Indeed, the sender's boss, whom he had inadvisably copied into his reply, was quickest to the draw. Within an hour, the sender was on the phone apologizing if his 'sense of humour' had been taken the wrong way.

A few lessons there:

Firstly, words fail to convey the same 'sense of humour' as a twinkle in the eye, wry smile or even mischievous tone in the voice.

Secondly, he may have thought his lightning-fast response was clever, but his boss and I disagreed.

The trouble with email is that it sends faster than our brains sometimes compute. That's why I always avoid replying online to a message that requires some delicacy. I need to see my reply complete, tinker, mull it over, sometimes seek a second opinion – and then send it.

Since the Egyptians created paper from papyrus, people have bottled out of saying what they mean face-to-face. Emails are today's letters. But, instead of chewing over the contents on the way to the post box, we need only hit a key to speak our minds.

Angry emails will cost jobs. So will careless ones. Ask Jo Moore!

We all must be aware that any email we send on certain topics could end up on the front page of a newspaper if sent to the wrong address, or if the recipient chooses to send it to the media. Therefore we should be able to explain and justify anything we write. And that was the difficulty Jo Moore had.

I was recently reminded just how blunt words can look when some players in an emergency exercise my company took part in took offence at our conclusions. Our client had commissioned us to create a media team to test the communications skills of all the agencies involved. The clients were happy with the conclusions, including the criticisms and recommendations. They had our written report, but we had also discussed the major points at length, face-to-face. However, when some of the other players received our written report, they reacted badly – and told us what they thought!

We decided that, next time round, we would present a video on the conclusions, so the points could be made visually, audibly and verbally. The following year, the video worked a treat. Instead of criticism being contained only in words, the video was more like a face-to-face meeting.

Whether in a written report or an email, be sure you can justify what you've written, before somebody else asks you to. By all means communicate at the speed of a bullet. Just avoid being the person who's fired.

The same, of course, applies to text messaging. A friend's teenage son was dating two girls at the same time. They happened to know each other but were unaware of his double-dealing. So, when Chris asked Vicky to the pictures, he crudely added to his text message '**Don't** tell Anna'. **(Pink Elephant!)**

His secret would have been safe, but for the fact that he scrolled down his address book and, because the last word of the message was 'Anna', he mistakenly sent the message to Anna.

Needless to say, a reply came back from his longer-term girlfriend Anna pointing out that he had sent the message to the wrong person. We can only speculate as to the damage done by that particular text message which turned out to be a boomerang, rather than a bullet.

The Queen's English

Some will argue that emails and text messaging are conspiring to destroy the very fabric of the English language.

Now, the correct way to speak, I was taught at school, was to use the Queen's English. But that was in the 1960s: an era when you had to be white to vote in America, when people were hanged in Britain even though some were innocent, when gay people could be prosecuted for having sex together and when children were beaten in schools because they were left-handed.

As with these discredited practices, I would suggest there is now a better alternative to the Queen's English. After all, the way we communicate has changed dramatically since Queen Elizabeth took the throne in 1952. Just compare the stiff, formalized television of that era to the way news is presented today.

The earliest BBC TV newsreaders were just that – readers unseen by the cameras. But their type of English was high society cocktail party English.

BBC news bulletins today remain more formal than their commercial TV counterparts. Yet they have loosened up enormously. An item may start 'Much of Britain's suffering a third day of flooding.' Of course, the Queen's English I was taught at school would have forbidden 'Britain's' and insisted on 'Britain is …'

But the former is how we would say it and that's the best way to hear it also.

It was the first lesson I was taught when I joined Radio Clyde in Glasgow in 1980 as a reporter. My then boss Alex Dickson told me 'You've been writing for the eye to read in newspapers so far. Now you have to write for the ear to hear. And it must be understood first time. You can re-read a paragraph in a newspaper. But on radio, it's gone forever.'

Since then, for radio and TV, I've written for the ear. So 'I have' becomes 'I've'. 'There will be' becomes 'there'll be' and 'the Government is' becomes 'the Government's'. And so on.

It's a habit that spills into my writing style, as you may have noticed. This really annoyed a former secretary who changed all my colloquial English in letters to clients back into the Queen's English. 'That's how I was taught at college,' she would tell me.

'Fine,' I would reply. 'But after a friendly chat with a client on the phone, why stiffen up in a letter reiterating the same point when informal English keeps the tone lighter?'

Constantly, she formalized my letters. Constantly, I deformalized her corrections.

It's the single biggest reason why business presentations sound stiff. The speech may have been well written – as written English, that reads well to the eye. But when read to an audience, it sounds stiff and formal, immediately making the speaker sound old-fashioned, perhaps a guardian of the Queen's English. The Queen herself now sounds extremely old-fashioned in her

Christmas Day Address. And while many attempts have been made to lighten up the broadcast, it's the written English and delivery style that make it sound stiff.

Is grammar important? Well, while grammar used to be taught rigidly, it has slipped lower and lower down the priorities of many schools – even disappearing in some quarters. Today, we've all learned in different ways and are most often comfortable with a form of grammar close to our own. Most people would put sincerity and credibility ahead of grammar.

And what of accents? Clients tell me each day how self-conscious they are of their Aberdeen/Liverpool/Newcastle accents. It tells me only where they've lived in their lives. If their voice is clear and confident, if they use the 'rules' I've debated at length here, their accent will be unimportant, compared to their confidence.

In Britain, attitudes to accents changed throughout the 1980s. I well remember arriving at the studios of ITN (Independent Television News) in London to do a couple of shifts there, while full-time at Scottish Television. Beside the Oxford and Cambridge-educated accents of their presenters, I really did feel as if I had parachuted in from a remote corner of Scotland.

But only six years later, when beginning work on BBC *Breakfast News* with Jill Dando and Nick Witchell, I felt completely at home. Two things had happened: my self-confidence had grown and 'regional' accents, as the BBC liked to call them, were now being encouraged across national TV.

So it became cool to have a Welsh, Northern Irish, Newcastle or Midlands accent, even my own Scots accent! That's when employers of telephone operators in call centres realized that these accents were often friendly and reassuring – hence the growth of call centres demanding such accents.

Language, like the earth itself, is ever changing, ever evolving. Yet I still bristle when I hear 'howlers', as I see them, in bulletins:

- Firstly, *fewer* describes a number while *less* describes a quantity. I can have *fewer* apples than you, but you may have *less* sugar. It's wrong, therefore, to talk about *less* apples as it is to describe *fewer* sugar.

- Secondly, a witness can *imply* that someone was at a crime scene and a jury can *infer* the same thing. However, just as the jury is unable to *imply* what the witness meant, neither can the witness *infer* it.

- Finally, *between* refers to two parties. We can have talks *between* British and French leaders. But if the Germans were involved, the talks would be *among* the three leaders.

So how important are all these subtleties? Well, to many people, they are unimportant. But just remember that the use of the wrong word or phrase interrupts the thought process in the listener's mind, often causing the audience to miss the next bit. The same goes for bad grammar.

So when you hear that '*less* holidaymakers visited...' you may be correcting the poor English used, while missing exactly where the declining numbers of holidaymakers visited.

(By the way, it is a *number* of holidaymakers, rather than a *quantity*. That's also often misused.)

Summary

1   *Emails travel at the speed of bullets, so be certain of what you're saying before pulling the trigger.*

2   *Conversational English makes a speech or presentation much easier to follow.*

3   *We all have accents. Stop being self-conscious about yours.*

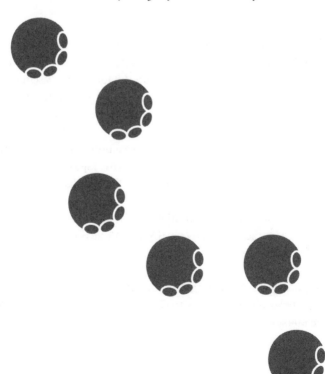

Chapter 12

Three Little Questions

'I know what I say at times is not very diplomatic.'
Nikita Khrushchev (Soviet Leader during the Cuban missile crisis)

Let's say a head teacher from the Cornish town of Truro scoops £10 million pounds on the lottery. How would the media cover that?

The local weekly newspaper would run it as their front page lead, with extensive coverage inside the paper, speaking to family, colleagues and pupils from the lucky man's school. The implications of the win, and the potential early retirement of a much-respected head teacher, would be covered extensively.

The regional radio station would give it prominence within their three-minute bulletin, but only after coverage of a fatal fire and local job losses, as well as the Chancellor's budget.

BBC TV news in London might run it as an 'and finally' story, giving it something between 15 and 45 seconds of airtime in a half-hour bulletin.

Why such a contrasting attitude? It's down to how important or interesting the story is to each audience. To the local paper's readership, it's huge. To the radio station's listenership, it's a strong local story. To the BBC's audience in Yorkshire, South Wales and Northern Ireland, it's of passing interest.

And that, in a nutshell, is how news agendas are organized.

So how should we determine our own agenda of news? In exactly the same way.

Our partner will be very interested in our pay rise, our children will be hard-pressed to notice the difference, our friends may be mildly pleased for us – and our distant friends, relatives and neighbours are unlikely even to be told.

We make these decisions every day, and we get many of them wrong, failing to realize how boring our news is to many people.

Remember Tom Watson's description of 'golf mouth'?

But 'golf mouth' can be applied to all sorts of situations, if given a different name. Going into minute detail about a new car – right down to the cubic capacity of the engine and how long it takes to do 0–60 miles an hour – would be 'car mouth'. A minute-by-minute account of our holiday would be 'holiday mouth'.

However, it's fair to say your non-golfing wife, husband or partner would like to know if you've won or lost your golf tie and your golf-mad son would want to know how you played and what went right or wrong. It all depends on the level of interest.

And that leads me back to journalism and three questions I should ask before writing my news story:

1   What do I want to say?

2   Who am I talking to?

3   So how should I explain it?

Let's put that in an everyday situation. Let's say you want a Friday off work to attend a wedding. The trouble is that the workload is heavy and the office is already under pressure. Would it be wise to say to your boss 'I know it's busy but I've been invited to a wedding next Friday and I'm sure you'll **not** even notice I'm off.' **(Pink Elephant!)**

Try it if you like and let me know how you get on. Pity about the wedding. You would have enjoyed it!

Instead, it would be more reasonable to say 'I've been invited to a wedding next Friday. I know it coincides with our busiest time. So I wondered how you would feel – if I got through my workload by Thursday night – about me taking the Friday as a day's holiday. I'd love to be at the wedding and I'd really appreciate if you could help me with this.'

The answer, by the way, may still be 'no'. But the first approach would increase the chances of that knock-back, while the second would reduce them.

So to answer our three questions …

1   What do I want to say? *I want to go to a wedding next Friday.*

2   Who am I talking to? *My hard-pressed boss.*

3   So how should I explain it? *By offering a solution and asking for his help.*

Communication often falters because we know what we want to say but completely fail to consider our audience. Yet, if we've ever talked to children – and parents should be masters at this – it should be very clear to us that it's *only* when we consider the audience that we can hope to communicate properly. And sometimes that goes badly wrong.

I heard how a mother alarmed her seven-year-old daughter while driving north over the Forth Road Bridge from Edinburgh to Fife. Pointing to the impressive Forth Rail Bridge to her right, she said 'On Saturday your Aunt Jill will bring you back home across that bridge. That'll be fun won't it?'

The girl looked at the rail bridge and fell silent. When her mum next looked, she could see tears streaming down her daughter's cheeks.

'What on earth's the matter?' she asked.

The girl could hardly talk for sobbing, having misinterpreted the purpose of the massive, twin-peaked rail bridge. 'I **don't** want to go away up there and away down there,' she sobbed. **(Pink Elephant!)** 'I feel sick on roller-coasters.'

You will know several people who fail to question what impact their words will have on the audience.

A relative of mine, thinking he was complimenting a young waitress who had shed many pounds on a diet, announced to my wife and me, in front of the young woman 'This is the waitress I was telling you about who used to be really fat.' Her face betrayed what she thought of that remark!

I was driving along the motorway one day, listening to a BBC Radio Four current affairs programme when a live interview touched on the subject of women priests in the Church of England. When a clergyman who had just voted against the proposal to have women priests was asked to justify his decision, I listened up for some good, old-fashioned controversy.

His answer was slow and deliberate: 'Because, it's ecumenically disingenic ...' And that's as far as I got before switching to the news on Radio Five Live, which at least I could understand.

The situation also made me ask myself if he even knew what he wanted to say. My perception is that we're often less sure than we would make out.

People are much better today than they were when answering machines and voicemail were introduced.

One former colleague of mine was so disorganized in his thoughts that the time allowed for a lengthy message had normally expired before he reached the key point. He would cry out in exasperation, before phoning back and having a stab at a more concise message.

Saturday night football phone-in programmes are littered with frustrated presenters asking incoherent fans 'What's your point, caller?'

Now, in phoning a radio station or leaving a message on voice-mail, we do know whom we're calling and so some level of organization of thoughts is expected. But what happens when you bump into an old school friend in a shop, only to be asked 'So what have you been doing since we left school?'

Where do you start? With your marriage – or your divorce? With the birth of your daughter – or her wedding? With your first job after leaving school – or your present one?

In all likelihood, you'll probably talk about what you've been doing that day, where you now work and who you now live with. But who knows? The question is so wide that the answer can go anywhere. And all because you were completely unprepared for the question.

So let's put some structure into our conversation, starting with what it is we want to say.

What do I want to say?

Often we're simply disorganized in what we want to say, hence the rambling answer machine messages. That's also why we walk away from an argument, suddenly remembering all the points we could have made.

So before lifting the phone, before addressing a meeting, before speaking to a shop assistant, work out what it is you want to say.

On our media training courses, there is a vast difference between the first interview we put participants through and the second. That's because we ask them to do the first interview before preparing any thoughts. But we insist that they write down three or four bullet points before the second interview – and then they have the chance to say what they really wanted to.

Yet some people are unable to tell you much about their job or company, other than the job title and a whole load of jargon that enshrouds it in mystery.

Therefore the second point is important:

Who am I speaking to?

The way you speak to your dad should be different to the way you speak to your children, which is different from the way you speak to your partner. Colleagues are another category, then there are friends, clients, suppliers – the list goes on. I say it's different because of the fact that each person is a different human being, with different interests and aspirations.

Even the place where somebody lives gives him or her a perspective different to others.

I once suggested to a network TV weather forecaster that, when she pointed to her map and said 'up in Scotland it'll remain cloudy, with showers across in Wales and down in Cornwall …', her references were only right from a London perspective. But those of us 'up' in Scotland, 'across' in Wales and 'down' in

Cornwall believed we were at the centre of the universe. From Scotland, Wales is 'down'. From Cornwall, Wales is 'up'. So 'across' is wrong each time! Next day she was back on GMTV, again niggling the Celts with some insensitive geographical references ...

I had to avoid the audience perspective trap myself while presenting to all parts of the UK from BBC *Breakfast News* in London.

On one occasion, my co-presenter Justin Webb asked how I felt the England/New Zealand Rugby World Cup semi-final would go that weekend. 'Well the heart says England,' I began, 'but in their current form, I'm afraid the head says the All Blacks should win.'

I phoned a producer at BBC Scotland shortly after the programme. Before discussing the football coverage we were arranging, he wanted to pull me up. 'You got your words all mixed up this morning,' he teased.

'How was that?' I asked, puzzled.

'You suggested you wanted England to beat New Zealand,' he explained. 'You must have meant it the other way round.'

I had a simple question for him: 'If an English presenter had been asked in the Glasgow studio whether Scotland would beat New Zealand, how would the Scottish audience react to him wishing for a Scottish defeat?' More than 80 per cent of my *Breakfast News* audience would be English. Watching from Scotland, it's easy to forget that.

Which leads me to the final question:

So how should I put it?

And this is the crucial one. If it's to a five-year-old who's upset at her dad going to London, it has to be with understanding and a bright picture of the benefit to her. If it's to a woman in your seat in the plane, it's with consideration for her embarrassment and understanding of the mix up. If it's to members of a workforce worried about their future, it's with sympathy for the job losses, explanation of the situation and confidence about the future, once the difficult decisions are made.

These three little questions are the backbone of any structured conversation, presentation or debate. Put them in place and communication becomes very much easier, by looking at the importance of your points and the order in which you should explain them.

Summary

1   *What do I want to say?* Always have a few points ready.

2   *Who am I speaking to?* Consider your audience and their in-terests.

3   *How should I put it?* Once you consider that, you can arrange your bullet points in order of importance.

Create Deeper Understanding

Chapter 13

Listen First to Understand

'Big people monopolize the listening. Small people monopolize the talking.'
David Schwartz

One of the greatest compliments anybody can pay you is to tell you that you are a great listener.

To be bothered to listen to other people, you have to be interested in what they have to say. And that's where many of us fall down. You will have seen poor listeners in action for yourself. Some ask you a question, pay attention to the first sentence of your answer and gradually become more distracted as the answer continues.

I was on a coffee break at a conference where exactly this happened. The person who had asked me the question saw someone he had to speak to and, without saying anything to me, just wandered off barely 20 seconds into my reply. I must have set a world record for audience boredom, without even getting as far as describing my last round of golf!

Other poor listeners nod diligently at what you're saying but are only really waiting for you to draw breath to tell you their own story. You could finish your sentence '… and so I chopped my wife's head off before leaving for work' and they would still tell you their story, oblivious to what you had just said.

And then there's the 'that's nothing compared to what happened to me' brigade, whose skill is in 'topping' your story. Their experience was bigger, richer, faster, more dangerous, funnier than yours, so you may as well accept that they will use you only as a ladder to climb higher in the conversation.

Finally, there are those who can be in your company for several hours and they will know nothing about you, because they failed to ask you a single question in that time. I'm always bemused when I come off the golf course, knowing all about my opponent's family, business, last holiday, next holiday – yet they can tell me nothing about my life, because of a failure to ask questions.

Of course, some people are genuinely shy and wonder what questions to ask. I tend to ask people about their family they have, what line of work they're in or where they live. I ask if they've been away on holiday this summer, or if they will get a chance before the winter.

Listening and asking questions becomes easy when you make it a habit. Men struggle a bit more with this than women, generally. However, some of the most successful men I know are great listeners. They pay attention to what you say. They take a deep and genuine interest in your life.

And if someone takes an interest in your life, you feel inclined to take an interest in theirs.

I was flying home from London a few years ago when I struck up a conversation with the man next to me. As we landed, he suddenly stopped and said 'My goodness, we've been deep in conversation all the way from London and I've just been talking about myself. What a bore!'

'On the contrary,' I replied. 'I already know all about me. I really enjoyed listening to what you had to say.'

And when he did ask about my career, I sensed he was genuinely interested, as I had been genuinely interested in his.

A few years ago, we heard the wife of an acquaintance of ours had died. We asked him round for supper a couple of weeks later and talked for hours. When he was leaving, he thanked us for supper and told us it had been good to catch up on all our news.

The thing is, our news failed to make it on to the agenda that evening. We had only talked about his wife, his daughter and what he would be doing to adjust to his new situation. But then, that had been the purpose of the evening. We had invited him round to listen to him.

We can all be cautious about contacting someone whose close relative or partner has just died, or calling a business colleague who's going through a bad patch. In reality, most people in these circumstances want to talk to someone who will listen empathetically, without offering quick-fix solutions to their problems.

I put this to the test with friends whose business had dramatically collapsed, burying their retirement plans in the rubble. On the phone, I simply wanted to know if they would like to meet to talk. We spent the following evening discussing events, even managing a few laughs along the way. Again, our role was to listen. But then that's what friends do when you're having a rough time.

Despite being a journalist since the age of 17 and a broadcaster from 21, I reckon that, once I had covered the basic questions, I was a poor listener until a few years ago.

I talked for a living.

But, in grasping the issues facing clients, I had to listen much better than I had previously done. Only when I listened first to understand could I hope to be understood in what I suggested to improve their communication.

Also, watching the way my wife listens has shown me just why people come to Caroline when they need someone to be supportive. She's a great listener.

As a nation, I believe we're much too quick to jump to conclusions because of what we believe a situation to be. We delve into our box of stereotypical views instead of listening in depth to what someone has to say in order to understand where they're coming from.

Listening is the key to understanding. Only when you learn to listen can you hope to understand.

Pay attention to the percentages – 55, 38 and 7

So now we understand that we must listen first, how do we go about convincing people of our ideas?

Well, if you really wanted to convince a friend to help you with a project, would you:

a   write to her

b   phone her

c   visit her

The answer becomes more obvious when you realize that only seven per cent of our message comes across in the words we choose, 38 per cent in the tone of our voice and 55 per cent in our body language, principally the look on our face.

So a meeting is more powerful than a phone call, which in turn is more powerful than a letter, email or text message.

This whole book is dedicated to selecting the right words – and they only account for a pathetic seven per cent of the message in any face-to-face conversation! (Of course, in a letter, email or text, they are 100% of the communication.)

Yet the foundations of a high-rise block of flats account for only a small percentage of the structure. However, if they are faulty, the building may collapse. So words are the crucial foundations of our communication tower block.

Now 38 per cent is a huge chunk of the message determined by tone, but just think for a minute about how one word can have a great variety of meanings:

- 'Yes' can be said politely by a shopkeeper, asking how he can help the next customer.

- 'Yes?' can be a demand from an irritated Basil Fawlty, meaning 'what do you want now?'

- 'Yes!' can be the shout from the sofa as your team nets the winning goal in injury time.

- 'Yes' can prove embarrassing, as Meg Ryan's character Sally demonstrated in a restaurant in the film *When Harry Met Sally*, as she groaned it louder and louder, to the discomfort of Billy Crystal's character Harry.

Tone is hugely important. But now consider all the permutations for 'yes' when adding a raised eyebrow, an angry frown or a jubilant smile. So body language wins out over tone and words.

That's why television, delivering us pictures, has dominated the media since its invention. Of course, radio did the same before TV. And when we had only newspapers, they were kings of the castle.

Our communications options are now so wide and varied that in one day we may text, email, send a letter, make a few phone calls, talk to people face to face, watch TV, listen to radio, read a newspaper and check out the weather forecast on the interactive satellite channel.

But however diverse these forms of communication become, they still split into just three categories.

If you can get the *words* right, your foundations are strong. They will help you find the right tone, because certain words adopt a certain tone – like positives, instead of negatives.

Finding the right *tone* can be difficult. To do so, we often have to fight emotions that can make us feel negative, although we're using positive words with our children. So well-chosen and positive words can still sound like a row unless the tone matches the words.

However, even if we overcome both these hurdles, *body language* is still waiting for its moment to catch us out. When we say that someone said all the right things but 'he still gave me the creeps', it tends to be body language rather than a sixth sense that gave the game away.

That's why I suggest that the aim with all communication is to be genuine. Otherwise, body language will more than likely find us out.

The strongest element of body language is good eye-contact. When someone looks you in the eye while telling you good news or bad, you trust them. When their eye-contact continues to falter, you have doubts. There are all sorts of reasons for poor eye-contact, shyness being one of them. But to win trust, we have to learn to overcome these obstacles. And when speaking to a group of several people round a table, I make sure I spread the eye-contact evenly and linger on each person for a few seconds, to involve them more in the conversation.

A clip of an interview on television recently reminded me of an incident that highlighted how important the percentages are. It was of Kevin Keegan, manager of Newcastle United in the mid-90s, rising to the bait of a comment thrown his way by the Manchester United manager Sir Alex Ferguson. The two teams were neck-and-neck in an exciting championship race when Fergie made a throwaway comment that Leeds United – due to play Newcastle – would give their north-east rivals an easier time than they had given Man United.

I remember reading Kevin Keegan's reaction in the papers at the time and remarking to my colleague that he sounded niggled. 'Niggled?' he replied. 'You should have seen him on television last night. He was incandescent with rage!'

Now that I've watched Keegan's reaction, and heard the tone of his voice, I can see exactly why the newspaper comment failed to capture his anger.

So, when it comes to your own message, remember the percentages: seven per cent (words), 38 per cent (tone) and 55 per cent (body language). They will determine your ability to convince one person, a meeting or a conference of a thousand people.

Or they may just betray the passion that your reported comments missed.

Summary

1   *Listen carefully to the person you're talking with.*

2   *Contribute to the conversation in a meaningful way, rather than just waiting to butt in.*

3   *Use body language and the tone of your voice to add conviction to your well-chosen words.*

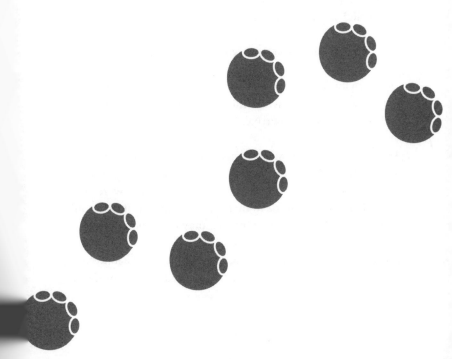

Chapter 14

Powerful Words

'Words are, of course, the most powerful drug used by mankind.'
Rudyard Kipling

You may have noticed that each chapter of this book has started with an appropriate quote to summarize part of the message. Most are there to add credibility to the advice that follows. And where the source is well-respected, the suggestion is that if that's their belief, it's likely to be right.

So when you borrow a quote, you borrow a reputation.

I've often found that powerful words can be just what's required to pick somebody up when they feel like giving up, or to put their setback into perspective.

A favourite of mine is *'failure is the point when you give up trying'*. Or put another way, *'success is getting up one more time than you've been knocked down'*. I've used these two with people who were going through a terrible trauma in their lives, wondering if they could ever succeed. By simply carrying on, they were succeeding.

One I found useful when feeling as if I was fighting a lone battle against an injustice concerning a friend – and wondering if I was doing the right thing – was *'It is necessary only for the good man to do nothing for evil to triumph.'*

When I heard these words, I determined that I would see the issue to its conclusion. That conclusion turned out to be a seven-year jail term for a sex abuser who had previously gone unpunished. The value of such sayings is to put your plight into perspective. It demonstrates that others have been there before you.

Whether in passing on advice or constructing a convincing presentation, be willing to dip into the experience of others to make the point.

Many of the principles to be found in this book can be found wrapped up in great quotes.

George Bernard Shaw on being proactive in life:

> *'People are always blaming their circumstances for what they are. I don't believe in circumstances. The people who get on in this world are the people who look for the circumstances they want, and if they can't find them, make them.'*

Abraham Lincoln on flushing out the watering down words:

> *'By all means, don't say "If I can"; say "I will."'*

Henry Ford on Pink Elephants:

> *'Whether you think you can or think you can't, you are right.'*

Oprah Winfrey on talking positively about yourself:

'When I look into the future, it's so bright it burns my eyes.'

Kenneth Tynan on negative criticism:

'A critic is a man who knows the way but can't drive the car.'

Sydney J. Harris on keeping things in perspective:

'When I hear someone sigh "Life is hard", I'm always tempted to ask "Compared to what?"'

George S. Clason on keeping it simple:

'Desires must be simple and definite. They defeat their own purpose should they be too many, too confusing, or beyond a man's training to accomplish.'

Thomas Fuller on failure to listen:

'None is so deaf as he that will not hear.'

Thomas Jefferson on keeping to the moral high ground of the Louisiana Highway:

'Whenever you are to do a thing, though it can never be known to yourself, ask how you would act were all the world looking at you.'

History is littered with speeches built on powerful words that marked a change in attitudes, a new beginning.

Abraham Lincoln on his quest to end slavery:

> *'A house divided against it cannot stand. I believe this government cannot endure permanently, half slave and half free.'*

Winston Churchill on becoming Britain's wartime Prime Minister in 1940:

> *'I have nothing to offer but blood, toil, tears and sweat.'*

John F. Kennedy in his inaugural address as President in 1961:

> *'And so, my fellow Americans: ask not what your country can do for you; ask what you can do for your country. My fellow citizens of the world: ask not what America will do for you, but what together we can do for the freedom of man.'*

Martin Luther King Jr on civil rights in 1963:

> *'I have a dream that my four little children will one day live in a nation where they will not be judged by the colour of their skin but by the content of their character.'*

(Pink Elephants were a way of life in those rhetorical times!)

Only Churchill lived to be old – Lincoln, Kennedy and King falling to the bullets of assassins. Words can change history. They can also pose such a threat to extremists that they lead to the premature death of the more moderate speaker.

I'll leave the last word to President Kennedy. It's a note of caution about empty words:

> *'Words alone are not enough. Where our strength and determination are clear, our words need merely to convey conviction, not belligerence. If we are strong, our strength will speak for itself. If we are weak, words will be of no help.'*

The profound irony of these words is that they were left unsaid. They should have been delivered by the President on November 22nd, 1963 in Dallas – the day John F. Kennedy was assassinated.

Summary

1   *Powerful words can sum up a situation better than loose thoughts.*

2   *They can inspire you to succeed and to act in the knowledge that others have gone there before you.*

3   *Words have to be consistent with your actions – otherwise they are empty words.*

Chapter 15

Think, Talk, Act ... Then Tell the World

'There are some who speak one moment before they think.'
Jean de la Bruyère (1645–1696)

All the horror stories I've shared with you came about through my thoughtlessness.

Wishing the poor woman who sat each cold and wet evening in a car park pay booth a happy redundancy; calling an impatient elderly driver an 'old git'; launching an attack on a tired restaurateur who dared to give my daughter a row. These were the actions of someone quick to speak and slow to think.

I've learned from getting it wrong so often to take a more subtle approach to communication. It's very simple. First think, then talk, then act.

Now that may seem patently obvious. But when things have gone wrong, it's often because I spoke first, then acted – and then thought long and hard about the consequences of my actions.

The minimal effort it takes to apply a little bit of thought first has rewarded me time and time again – by quietly securing my seat in a plane when someone else is sitting in it; by knowing to say 'sorry' to a large tennis crowd who have missed part of the match through our mistake; by translating the complicated jargon of business into words that everybody can understand.

It takes practice to improve the way we communicate by applying the 'Highway Code' rules in this book. But I now find – because the principles are in place all the time – that getting my message across to everybody in my life is easier than it's ever been.

I clearly remember sitting in my dad's car on my 17th birthday, letting out the clutch and moving off. When I felt I was going to hit the first parked car 100 yards on, I really wondered if I would ever drive with confidence.

That was the summer I entered journalism. My driving experience and my communication experience have run along parallel lines ever since. In both, I've got myself into scrapes and done damage. I've also learned from each mistake.

But today, I drive with confidence, wherever I happen to be. And I talk with confidence to friends and strangers alike because of the Highway Code I follow. If you've driven for some time, you'll know what I mean. But the awareness of these communication rules may be entirely new to you.

Show that same spirit of adventure you showed in learning to drive – or in playing an instrument, or in climbing a mountain for the first time.

Follow this Highway Code for communication and feel your confidence grow. You will have setbacks. You'll catch yourself breaking the rules. But persist and the rewards will be enormous.

Following these rules, you can achieve what you want in life by choosing the right words at the right time.

How you make use of these principles is entirely up to you. Perhaps you'll regard this book simply as an interesting read. Or perhaps you'll dare to adopt my rules and make them yours. It's perfectly easy. Just try them one at a time and watch them work.

Start by erasing the Pink Elephants from your speech. Every time you're tempted to use a sentence with a 'not' or a 'don't' (or any 'n't' for that matter), convert it to a positive.

To begin with, you'll find yourself stumbling, half way through an 'I hope I **didn't** phone too late ...' **(Pink Elephant!)** before adding 'I just thought I'd call before you went to bed.'

You'll hear a colleague talking in total management-speak jargon and find yourself, for the first time, asking him to explain what he means. You may even offer him a series of pictures to replace the fog of abstract nouns he's thrown your way.

When a friend tells you her new partner is 'quite' caring, the temptation may be to ask her 'Just how caring is "quite"?'

When you're asked to complete a job by Friday, the phrase 'I'll do my best' will be vanquished, replaced by 'I'll see it's done.'

If you suffer a setback at work, Regret, Reason and Remedy will be waiting by your side to get you out of the swamp and back on the Louisiana Highway.

Impossible questions will be met with 'I don't know. I'll give that some thought and get back to you.' Impossible demands will be met with 'No, but I can have it finished next week.'

Critical emails will receive considered and polite responses. And you'll arrange to meet that person whose support you need to enlist, rather than send them an electronic message.

When asked to make a presentation, you'll structure your content by asking yourself: what do I want to say, who am I talking to – so how will I put it?

You'll speak with warmth and appropriate humour, with enthusiasm and great eye-contact. Your tone will convey conviction and your words will inspire.

And when your boss congratulates you on a successful presentation, you'll say 'Thank you. I was pleased with the reception. And thanks for giving me the opportunity to address the conference.'

I have experienced at first hand how these rules have enriched my life and the lives of others I've met.

The first time I discovered their power it was in a fraught meeting with a former TV boss. He clearly wanted me off a sports programme to make way for a regular member of staff who would require less of his already-stretched budget. But to every negative he threw my way – looking for a fight – I replied with a positive. After a 15-minute siege, I emerged from his office with my job still intact and retained it for a further two years until I decided to stand down.

That was in 1991. Four years later, I used every single rule I've mentioned in dealing with a media issue that dominated the tabloids throughout that summer and swallowed up hundreds of column inches in the broadsheets. It became a hot topic on radio and the subject of two major TV documentary programmes, networked by the BBC.

My wife and I stood up publicly for the TV comedy actor Eric Cullen (Wee Burney in *Rab C. Nesbitt*), after offensive material was removed from his house during a police raid. Our reason was very simple. He had been sexually abused from adolescence into early adulthood, then had seen his home used as a dumping ground for his abusers' porn, while they blackmailed him and extorted money during his new-found fame.

Handling the media through that summer – at his court case (where he was jailed) and up to the appeal (which we won) – was extremely difficult. The subject matter was sensitive and much misunderstood. But when the media pressure on the legal system helped to bring to justice one of his abusers, sending him to jail for seven years, it was all worthwhile. Eric, sadly, had died before then, but the media had helped us tremendously in bringing out the truth of his tragic story.

Interestingly, his abuser convinced the *Daily Express* to splash his conviction across page one with a single unwitting remark. As a photographer snapped him coming off a train to face the court, the abuser said 'I **never** abused Eric Cullen.' **(Pink Elephant!)** Eric's name had been removed from the court's list of abuse victims by this stage. But the Pink Elephant sealed his fate in public perception.

The climax of three years' work was an appearance on Esther Rantzen's BBC programme, allowing us – under her incisive cross-examination – the opportunity of setting all that had gone before in a constructive context.

Shortly after that, the case of the police detective Shirley McKie, whom I mentioned earlier was wrongly accused (and cleared) of perjury over false fingerprint evidence, sent us down a familiar path. This time, I gave Shirley the ammunition she required to deal with the media herself, by teaching her the rules.

In February 2006 – after a 9-year battle – Shirley was awarded £750,000 as compensation for the loss of her career by the Scottish Executive, who conceded the "mistake" over the fingerprint. She stuck to the truth, told her complicated story in plain English, and has kept her sanity, while many of her opponents attempted to undermine her.

The media was the only avenue open to Shirley to uncover the truth of her unique case. She believes she's now been interviewed close to 200 times by newspapers, radio and television, including three BBC *Panorama* special reports. Type her name into any Internet search engine and dozens of entries will testify to the infamy of her case and her courage in tackling it head-on. She has used our Highway Code as her principles in fighting for justice.

Her heart-warming personal battle is in sharp contrast to the story of a production plant when closure was announced. You would expect dejection and despair as the final day of production drew closer. Yet, following exactly the same principles of communication, United Distillers & Vintners achieved something quite remarkable several years ago when closing their

Gordon's Gin bottling plant at Laindon in Essex. Because of the honesty of their words, their commitment to help workers find new jobs and their integrity in doing exactly what they said they would do (and when), productivity in the final months actually rose. Morale was maintained to the end and a proud workforce took its professionalism into new jobs elsewhere.

If you have something of interest to say, tell as many people as you can. Interest and inspire them with your energy and enthusiasm.

I have turned to the media for publicity on the launch of golf and football videos I've produced, charity balls we have organized, football charities I've supported, children's charities I've been involved with, appeals I've fronted, blind golfers' societies of which I've been patron, a school merger I've agreed with, court action I've disagreed with. In fact, you may well have bought this book on the strength of a newspaper, radio or television article about it.

Each of these articles was free of charge. Certainly, I needed to know what I wanted to say, who I was speaking to and therefore how I had to put it. But the media offered me the megaphone if I was prepared to pick it up and use it.

The same opportunity exists for everybody. It just takes the application of our Highway Code to make the dealings with journalists constructive and well-organized.

Finally, you may question whether the words you choose really are a matter of life or death. So here's the story that proves that they can be.

In 1998, my clients Compaq (now Hewlett Packard) called to say they wanted me to carry out a very unusual media training course for an employee and her daughter. Later that week, I met Angela MacVicar and 19-year-old Johanna, who was suffering from leu-kaemia and required a bone marrow transplant. Compaq were hoping to create some publicity to seek a suitable bone marrow donor for Johanna, who would need to handle interviews.

It was the most emotional day's training I have ever conducted. Quite simply, I had to recondition this brave teenager away from talking up her chances, in order that she might tell the truth. She had to tell her audience, whoever they might be: 'Without a suitable bone marrow match, I will die.'

At the end of the session, I promised to help create publicity for an appeal, so I called Eamonn Holmes, my good friend and colleague from *Breakfast News* days. Two days later, Angela and Johanna sat on the GMTV couch being interviewed by the empathetic Irish-man, bravely and confidently telling their story. As Johanna told several million viewers 'Without a suitable donor, I will die,' I felt my eyes well up. But at the same time, I was both in awe of her courage and thrilled that she had got her message across.

More than ten thousand viewers called a help-line to offer support. Many eventually offered blood samples to see if they matched. At present, at least 20 people can now say that they were matched up with a suitable donor through Johanna's appeal, and that her ability to tell her story to the world saved their lives.

Through tireless campaigning, Angela and Johanna became friendly with top entertainer Robbie Williams, who furthered their appeal. At least one other person's life can now be saved, thanks to a match found through the singer's intervention. They also became close to actor Dougray Scott, who introduced them to one of the world's leading experts on Johanna's condition, who changed her medication – enabling her to feel fit enough to travel to Australia.

Sadly, in May 2005, Johanna lost her brave battle for life. At a memorial fund-raiser a year later, I spoke of the brilliant relay race she had run across the world in the name of the Anthony Nolan Bone Marrow Trust – and how, as close friends, we would continue the race carrying her baton.

Few people reading this will have had to play the cards dealt by life to Eric Cullen, Shirley McKie or Johanna MacVicar. Telling your story and reaching for your goals should be, in most cases, a journey less hampered by such obstacles.

So follow these principles when you're being interviewed for your next job. Stick to the rules when you're next speaking in public.

Take exactly the same approach when asking your local newspaper to publicize a charity run, church fete or fundraising ball. There is always at least one branch of the media that can help further your cause, while furthering its own. Be proactive, be clear and be enthusiastic.

The world's greatest basketball player, Michael Jordan took a breathtakingly honest view of his performances. He said 'I missed every basket that I never attempted.'

You may live to regret your missed opportunities. Instead, set your targets, choose your words and go for it. And if you miss, try again. And again.

Until you succeed.

Summary

1   *Put all the Highway Code rules of good communication into action each day.*

2   *Allow your confidence to grow from the certainty they bring to your words, your thoughts and your actions.*

3   *Tell the world what you have to offer. It can mean the difference between success and failure, happiness and frustration. Even life and death.*

What Do Your Words Say About You?

Twenty-one questions to self-test your communications skills at work and with friends.

1 Your partner tends to take offence when you criticize his dress sense … but his new shirt is hideous. Do you say:
   a 'I'm not saying it's hideous … just a little loud.'
   b 'Don't take offence, but you have better shirts.'
   c 'You look better in that other new shirt.'

2 Your boss asks you to present to senior colleagues about a project you're right behind. In the presentation, do you tell them:
   a 'I think this scheme will be tremendous.'
   b 'I firmly believe this scheme will be tremendous.'
   c 'I know this scheme will be tremendous.'

3 At the end of a frantic day at work, you and your colleagues are exhausted and rushing home. Do you say to them:
   a 'Thanks and well done everyone. We got through a power of work.'
   b 'Make sure you get to bed early. Tomorrow will be busier.'
   c 'Another day, another dollar.'

4 Your boss is pleased with your work and congratulates you in front of colleagues. Do you say:

   a 'Not at all. It was easy.'

   b 'I'm only doing my job.'

   c 'Thank you. I'm glad it went well.'

5 Your boss tells you and your colleagues that she will be implementing the new DTML system from next week. She may as well be speaking Martian, as you are clueless as to what she means. Do you say:

   a 'Looking forward to it. It'll make a big difference.'

   b Nothing. You just hope your colleagues can explain it to you later.

   c 'Excuse me. What is that?'

6 You have an important presentation to make to colleagues, some of them very senior and others new recruits. Do you:

   a Use the company jargon to show your bosses you know the script.

   b Use simple language for the new recruits … at risk of your bosses feeling patronized.

   c Throw in a little company jargon to satisfy everyone.

7 You've been asked to give a written reference for a friend's son. However, you know he is constantly late for work. Do you:

   a Under the 'punctuality' column write: 'One weakness that needs some work.'

   b Refuse to give the reference, without explaining why.

   c Use woolly words to cover his poor punctuality.

8   Your child or partner asks to be picked up at the station at 9 p.m. You're able to do it, but know you'll only start the ten-minute journey once *Who Wants to be a Millionaire?* finishes at 9. Do you say:
    a   'I'll do my best to be there at 9.'
    b   'I'll try to be there at 9.'
    c   'I'll be there at 10 past 9.'

9   Your friend asks you to the cinema to see the latest Austin Powers film, although you would far rather see the new Harry Potter film. Do you say:
    a   'No, but I would go with you to see Harry Potter.'
    b   'Yes, that will be great.' (And suffer through the film in silence.)
    c   'That's fine.' (Then call off 'sick' on the day.)

10 Over dinner, your friend says all terrorists should be executed without trial. You disagree strongly, so do you say:
    a   'You're entirely wrong.'
    b   'Your argument makes no sense to me.'
    c   'I take a different view entirely.'

11 You're good at getting on with other people and quick on the computer. Your boss asks if you can help train some colleagues by demonstrating your knowledge on the keyboard. Do you say:
    a   'Yes, I'll do that.'
    b   'Hopefully I'll manage to do that.'
    c   'I'm reasonably sure I can do that.'

12 Over dinner, your friend asks you in front of people you know less well what you think of America's policy on the Middle East. You're worried about showing your ignorance, so do you:

a Waffle with conviction.

b Say you can see both the Israeli and Palestinian point of view (even though you know neither).

c Say: 'I really don't know for sure what America's policy is.'

13 You're set a deadline to complete a piece of work within one week. Even if you worked all weekend and several evenings, you know the work requires a fortnight. Do you say:

a 'I'll see it's done on time.' (Knowing you'll have to make excuses next week.)

b 'I'll need more help/more time/both if I'm to make that deadline.'

c 'The deadline's impossible. I'm already overworked.'

14 In a pub, a colleague … after a few drinks … criticizes your taste in men. Do you tell her:

a 'At least I have men in my life.'

b 'You're hardly one to throw stones.'

c 'My taste is my business, as yours is yours.'

15 You want a friend to help you with a considerable chunk of his time to organize a charity event. It's a while since you've seen him, so do you make your request:

a By arranging to meet up to discuss it.

b By sending an email to save time.

c By asking for help during a phone call.

16 You want lots of people to buy tickets for your charity event (now your friend is helping) and decide to approach your local newspaper. Do you:
   a Phone the local paper and ask if they've heard about it.
   b Write the key points down and explain them to a reporter.
   c Tell the reporter all about it and ask to see the story before it's published to check for inaccuracies.

17 A friend's mother has just died. Should you:
   a Meet her for a coffee to offer her advice.
   b Leave it for a month to give her time to reflect.
   c Contact her to listen to how she's been coping.

18 You receive a critical email demanding an immediate explanation as to why something at work has gone wrong. Do you:
   a Acknowledge receipt of the email, explain that you'll check some facts then reply in full when you have them.
   b Reply instantly with your 'gut' feeling about the issue.
   c Meet fire with fire ... and reply with a zinger.

19 In a row with your partner, he accused you of failing to pass on a phone message ... which you denied. On reflection, you now know he was right. You had simply forgotten about the call (which he has done in the past himself). Do you say:
   a 'I was in the wrong ... for once.'
   b 'We're both as bad as each other.'
   c 'I'm sorry, I was wrong.'

20 If you've now admitted that you were wrong, how do you repair the situation? Do you:
   a Tell him that you're always getting things wrong and that it's just the way you are.
   b Tell him that you were happy to say sorry this time ... but you'll remind him of the apology next time he's in the wrong.
   c Say you're sorry ... you had forgotten about the call ... and you've put a pen and pad by the phone for each of you to write down messages.

21 You are unhappy with the behaviour of one of your colleagues. Do you:
   a Tell your other colleagues privately (while he's out) why you're unhappy with him.
   b Ask to see him privately and tell him why you're unhappy.
   c Confront him in front of others to teach him a lesson.

Answers

1 Answer: c
Both other statements are Pink Elephants (unnecessary negatives) that only reinforce the words 'hideous' or 'offence'. Answer 'c' avoids that trap yet tells the truth.

2 Answer: b
'I think' is only a thought and sounds woolly. 'I know' can sound arrogant, when it's impossible to know for certain about the future. 'I firmly believe' is a statement on your firm belief, the best indication of a commitment to success.

3   Answer: a

'Thank you and well done' when said genuinely, can be the most encouraging words in the English language. Most people report that they feel undervalued at work and that they are seldom, if ever, thanked for busting a gut. If so, why should they bother tomorrow?

4   Answer: c

When you reject praise ... often for fear of looking 'big-headed' ... you deny your confidence the chance to grow. Accept it. Bank it. And draw on that reserve of praise and confidence if something goes wrong the next time.

5   Answer: c

Your boss will want you to understand. She may have forgotten that she is yet to explain the new system to you. While you may feel stupid at having to ask, who will feel stupid if the system fails because everybody was confused?

6   Answer: b

Use of any jargon will leave the new recruits baffled, unable to follow what you're saying. Keeping it simple will demonstrate that you can interpret a complicated message, helping everyone to understand. A rare skill!

7   Answer: a

Refusal to write a reference is running away from an issue that could be addressed. Covering up for his bad time-keeping would now bring your integrity into question.

Only telling the truth will maintain your integrity.

8   Answer: c

'I'll do my best' and 'I'll try' demonstrate a lack of certainty and commitment. They leave your partner or child unsure if you'll be there on time. Be clear … and be there.

9   Answer: a

Why waste your money and time or suffer the guilt of telling a lie to your friend? By saying 'no', you're asserting a view on a film, but showing that you would enjoy going to the cinema with your friend.

10   Answer: c

The other two answers are unnecessarily provocative because of the words 'you' and 'your'. If you want to win the debate, argue against the view, rather than the person.

11   Answer: a

'Hopefully' and 'reasonably' are giving you a get-out clause in case you fail. You're good with people, good with the computer and trusted by your boss. Just do it … without the 'watering down' words.

12   Answer: c

The reality is that what we don't know completely outweighs what we do know about the world. Why pretend and dig yourself into a hole? Tell the truth and people will respect your honesty.

13   Answer: b

Setting yourself up for failure or throwing the problem back in your boss's face are both unhelpful routes. Deal with the issue … and the solution … right away.

14   Answer: c

If you reply with an insult, you've lost the moral high ground. The third answer is a statement of fact, rather than an opinion. While your colleague may regret her words when she sobers up, you must also look her in the eye the next day and be able to hold your head high.

15   Answer: a

If you really want help and it involves sacrifice on your friend's part, it's much easier to persuade him face-to-face. Emails can look cold and may be overlooked ... and it's easier to say 'no' on the phone.

16   Answer: b

Local newspapers thrive on local stories about local people. They're likely only to hear about it if you tell them. But they're short of time and want to get the facts right, so make it easy to understand. However, let them get on with their job and avoid treating them like a child by asking to see their work.

17   Answer: c

Most people (although not all) will welcome the chance to talk and just be listened to. Advice from your perspective may be irrelevant. Your friend may also question where you were when she needed you there for her.

18   Answer: a

'Gut' feelings may prove entirely wrong and replying with criticism brings you down to the level of the critic, when you may have been blameless in the first place. The only way to retain the moral high ground is with a quick acknowledgement and a considered reply, based on facts.

19 Answer: c
Qualified apologies are unsatisfactory. Swallow your pride, accept your mistake and apologize.

20 Answer: c
Regret, (I'm sorry I was wrong); Reason (I forgot I had taken the call); and Remedy (I've put a pad and pen by the phone for each of us) is the best and quickest way to repair the damage. Remember the Three Rs.

21 Answer: b
Talking behind his back is cowardly and criticizing him in public may give short-term satisfaction but will damage your integrity. Remember to criticize in private and praise in public ... and not vice versa.

Scoring: one point for every correct answer

21–16 points: You have great integrity and assert yourself well

15–10 points: Much room for improvement in the honesty and commitment of your words

9–5 points: Re-read this book at the first opportunity

4–0 points: Stay right there. Speak to nobody. I'll bring you a copy to memorize.

Index

Be an Advanced Pink Elephant Hunter

"For over 20 years I have been helping individuals and some of the world's leading organisations hunt out their Pink Elephants, improve presentation skills and handle the media more effectively. If you have benefitted from the ideas in this book then just imagine how your entire organisation could operate using these effective communication principles."

Bill McFarlan
Managing Director

Effective Communication Courses:

Drop the Pink Elephant Seminars
Engaging the Media Courses
Media Training
Advanced Presentation Skills Courses

Consultancy and Coaching:

We support business leaders in communicating change, dealing with the media and improving their communication skills.

Audio-Visual Production:

Our Audio-Visual Production division turns those communication principles into highly effective videos, DVDs, websites and interactive tools to help you get your message across.

For more information on improving your communications contact us today at the Broadcasting Business on +44 (0)141 427 2545 or visit www.broadcastingbusiness.co.uk